BLESSED BY ILLNESS

BLESSED BY ILLNESS

by
L.F.C. Mees, M.D.

Anthroposophic Press
Spring Valley, New York

The original Dutch edition of this work bears the title, *Geneeskunde op de Drempel*, and was first published in 1981. The translation from the Dutch for this volume was revised by Coralee Fredrickson and Alice Wulsin.

Copyright © 1983
by Anthroposophic Press

Library of Congress Cataloging in Publication Data

Mees, L. F. C.
  Blessed by illness.

  Translation of: Geneeskunde op de drempel.
  Bibliography: p.
  1. Anthroposophical therapy.   2.   Cancer—Treatment.
I.   Title.
RZ409.7.M4413   1983   610   83-15866
ISBN 0-88010-054-0

Cover design by Peter van Oordt

PRINTED IN THE UNITED STATES OF AMERICA.

A PERSONAL WORD TO THE READER

When approaching medical science, we meet a fascinating world with equally fascinating problems. Everyone who is acquainted with current events knows about these problems.

Medicine has always been concerned about illness and healing. Here, however, modern medicine has gone astray. It is my conviction that doctors have gradually forgotten about the true nature of illness as well as the true nature of healing. The contents of this book seek to justify this point of view.

The origin of this book goes back to a series of lectures I was asked to give at Emerson College, England on the subject, "Medicine in the Past, Present, and Future." Afterward a friend in the audience asked me to write down the contents of the course so as to inform a greater number of people about my approach. The purpose of this book, as will be shown extensively, is not to contradict modern methods of treatment but to show the way to a possible extension of medicine in the future.

L.F.C. Mees

Table of Contents

A Personal Word to the Reader   v

I. Setting the Stage: "Are We on the
   Right Path?"   1

II. Approaching the Issue   9
    Introduction   9
    Knowing and Believing   13
    A Characteristic of Medicine in the
    Beginning of the Twentieth Century   24

III. The History of Medicine   29
     EGYPT
        Healing in Early Times   29
     GREECE
        Medicine before Hippocrates   37
        Hippocrates—a Threshold   42
        An Important Interval   50
     EUROPE
        Medicine after Hippocrates   58
        Paracelsus, Van Helmont,
        Hahnemann   71
        The Nineteenth Century   76
        The Dramatic Transition to the
        Twentieth Century   80

IV. Toward an Extension of Modern Medicine . . .   93
    A Conversation   93
    A New Impulse in Medicine 101
    Anti-Forces   103

V. Considering Healing in a New Light 117
    THE ILLNESS
      Illness and Predisposition 117
      Inflammation and Cancer: a Polarity ... 132
      Illness and the Human Constitution 144
      Cancer and Psychosomatism 150
    THE PRACTICE OF HEALING
      Evolution in the Kingdoms of Nature ... 154
      The Kingdom of the Animals and
      Human Evolution 158
      The Kingdom of the Plants and
      Human Evolution 163
      The Kingdom of the Minerals and
      Human Evolution 169
      Special Minerals in our Environment ... 171
      Special Plants in our Environment 176
      The Prospect of Healing Cancer 182
    CHANGING OUR MINDS
      The Course of Human Life:
      A Consideration of Reincarnation 194
      Experiences in Daily Life 202
      Conditions for Healing in the Future ... 212
      A Recapitulation 232

VI. Epilogue 239

I

Setting the Stage: "Are We on the Right Path?"

In the fall of 1977, an article with the title, "Are We on the Right Path," by the Dutch professor, L.B.W. Jongkees, appeared in the principal journal of the Medical Society in Holland. The article contains two main points. The first is that doctors have entered into many activities that have become so great a burden that they cannot really fulfill their proper tasks. The second main point shows the astonishing results of medical treatment in the last fifty years and the achievements in so many realms of medicine. Jongkees wonders, however, why so many are looking for what is called alternative treatment. The article begins:

> For many centuries physicians considered it their task to care for the health of man. Sometimes this was spoken of as 'fighting illness.'
> . . . . . However, a problem concerning the concept of illness hardly existed.

Jongkees continues by considering the attacks on medicine, for instance by Dr. Illich, which gradually may become known all over the world, an attack that he calls one-sided and unjust. He speaks about society, which often shows hostility toward doctors. On the one hand all sorts of quacks are free to practice more and more, while

1

on the other doctors are increasingly threatened with
lawsuits by patients. He says that doctors themselves have
caused this partly with their own optimism at the success-
ful results of modern medicine. They did not foresee the
situation in which the patient himself would gain so
much influence. He gives some examples:

> Patients know about the existence of antibiotics and ask
> for them, even in cases where they should not be applied
> at all. Not only in the United States but also in Europe
> more and more people are coming to ask for their 'shot,'
> with the result that virus illnesses, pain, fever, paralysis,
> and headaches are being treated with antibiotics; worse,
> even doctors themselves are beginning to believe it!

In his article he writes further:

> It is striking that the great achievements in medicine,
> especially over the last fifty years, have not met that
> warm-hearted acknowledgement that might have been
> expected, especially as far as young students are con-
> cerned, and yet we cannot deny these achievements. We
> owe to modern medicine the decrease in infectious ill-
> nesses, our modern hygiene, antibiotics, and vaccinations.
> It is due to doctors in the first place that we have im-
> proved sewerage and water systems. Nobody can deny
> what medicine has meant in the fight against diabetes,
> scurvy, and all other avitaminoses. Indeed, medical suc-
> cess in the last century has been spectacular.
> In the realm of surgery, I may mention the advancements
> in heart surgery, plastic surgery, and micro-surgery. In
> the realm of internal medicine, besides the possibilities
> already mentioned, we must not forget immunology, the
> larger understanding in the realms of psychology and
> psychiatry, especially as developed by Freud, and the
> development of prostheses for eye illnesses, ear illnesses,
> and for the handicapped.

> Yet it is as if the appreciation for medicine and doctors is in inverse proportion to their undeniable success. People do not appreciate what has been achieved but reproach what has not been achieved . . . . But is it not partly our own fault? Have we 'guardians of health' not aimed too high? Have we not kept ourselves too close to the old maxim, "Do everything to lengthen life," while making life pleasant is also important in this time of possibility. Are we not too optimistic in trying to let everybody profit from as many new medicines as possible, failures included?
>
> In this way I could continue with questions that some will answer with yes, others with no. Some, perhaps, would not even dare to answer them at all. I think it is crucial to ask these questions, however—I hope for answers.

Jongkees is not the only medical authority who has shown concern about the situation in the realm of medicine. We will give some examples that support what is best expressed by this question, "Are we on the right path?"

The editor of another leading Dutch medical periodical* wrote an article in 1978 on alternative medicine, in which he said:

> Although it has done away with infectious illnesses and discovered favorable possibilities for treating many other ailments, modern medicine is confronted more than ever with illnesses for which official medicine has not yet found an answer.
>
> . . . . . .
>
> The general conviction is that if official medicine continues to be successful regarding treatments, the so-called alternative treatments will disappear by themselves. This,

---

*Dr. Bol, Chief Editor of *Medical Contact*, 1978.

however, is unlikely. Modern medicine has its results but also its limitations owing to its scientific thinking. Observation, the forming of theory and hypothesis, and reproduceable processes form a necessary chain in this way of thinking. The rest, to this way of thinking, is quackery. However, our society is confronted with seven million contacts between patients and healers who do not have a university education in medicine. This cannot be denied, either by the government or by the medical profession.

Another doctor* wrote an article called, "The Tragedy of the Seventies," in which he brought the following to our attention:

> Clinical medicine in the 'first world' (in the West) has in the last decades been confronted increasingly with two problems, the solution of which seems further off than ever, in spite of all efforts, inventiveness, and investigation: diseases of the blood vessels and carcinoma . . . After a period of hope for a solution to the problem of arteriosclerosis and heart disease through use of anticoagulents, we must deal with a vague feeling of disappointment about the achieved results. . .
>
> In spite of the incredible achievements of early diagnoses and the improvement in surgery, our understanding of the origin of carcinoma must be characterized as very primitive.

Something else must be mentioned as well, however. A well-known Dutch former Medical Inspector of Health, whose opinion still carries weight, recently remarked that the Arbitral Committee for Alternative

---

*Dr. F. van Soeren, doctor of internal medicine, *Medical Contact*, 1978.

Modes of Treatment ought to have stated that, beyond
the acknowledged medical science as studied at our universities, no effective methods of healing *could possibly
exist!*

His proud certainty reveals a viewpoint opposite to
that revealed in the quotations presented until now. We
should also keep in mind, however, that this opinion is
meant seriously, that such a person is convinced of the
blessings of modern medical science. We must also try to
understand his point of view and to look for an appropriate approach.

Returning to the article by Jongkees, we may find
that the thoughts expressed there are by no means surprising in themselves. They have been declared for many
years, in many places where people are dealing with
modern medical treatment. The reason I consider Jongkees' article so important is that it is *he* who writes it
openly in a leading Dutch medical journal. Jongkees represents the highest level of medical science in Holland. It
is not necessary for everyone to agree with him. The
openness and clarity with which he put forward his
thoughts and the earnestness that one feels behind them
—again from someone of his position—mean something
that I would like to characterize with the words: a door
has been opened; because it is *he* who has opened it, we
can truly add that *it can never be shut again.* As doctors
we need not remain silent any longer about problems,
doubts, even misgivings that live in so many hearts,
although often they remain unspoken.

We need no longer submit to the authority of medical
science. Above all, we should fight the paralyzing influence of one of the most dangerous powers in modern
time, which threatens to hold us in fetters: public opin-

ion. It is this that has created the word "alternative." We should forget about feeling "alternative" and learn instead how we can work together.

* * *

In this book many references will appear that generally are avoided in what are called scientific works. I bring in mythology, quotations from the Bible, and the insights of Rudolf Steiner (founder of the Anthroposophical Society). Regarding these I should like to ask the reader never to accept mythology or the Bible and never to believe what Rudolf Steiner said. Merely approach all these phenomena with an open mind. Listen to them and try to discover whether or not they make sense.

I have often lectured to audiences in which people continually were comparing what they heard with their own opinions. It was if they lectured to themselves in reverse, as if they followed the outline of my talk, which was at the same time the outline of their own silent lecture. The yes-no, agreeing-disagreeing, etc., could be felt. The two lines showed a perfect congruency that became obvious in the conversation and discussion afterward. The result was that there had been no exchange at all; nothing had been experienced in a new way.

If someone asks during a lecture, "To whom do you refer?" and you mention some name, generally he will be satisfied. We should understand, however, that it would be quite logical to ask; "Where did he, to whom I referred, get this information?" Should we not develop the courage to base a conviction on something in ourselves, understanding that man is that wonderful, earthly being that can give origin, that can be original?

What is important, while listening to someone else, is to do away—for the time being—with our own well-known pattern of thoughts, to bring to a standstill our usual trend of thinking, to open ourselves to another world of ideas, neither denying nor agreeing, only listening. I usually put this in a short sentence: "Don't Say No, Just Say Oh!"

The question is whether this will enable us to find a new approach to phenomena that are for us, at this moment, unsolved riddles. The more we follow this method, the more we will discover a light that will shine in the world of our thoughts. Besides, it will be a surprise to discover that revelations from the realms that have been mentioned before (mythology, the Bible, anthroposophy), if looked at in the appropriate way, will never contradict discoveries in the realm of exact science "looked at in the appropriate way." The facts in the world of matter are not materialistic. Facts are sacred. Only the way in which we think about them has created materialism.

II

Approaching the Issue

Introduction

One of the main problems with which we will be dealing regarding healing in the past, present, and future is the change in man's consciousness in the course of time. Generally people believe that in the past, even thousands of years ago, humanity thought, felt, and acted in about the same way as we do nowadays, albeit in a more-or-less primitive manner. One imagines man to have evolved out of the animal-state, to have developed the capacity to think some millions of years ago and, in a straight line, to have gathered the knowledge that he possesses today. If we look at the content of the spiritual life, however, the appearance and behavior of man in the course of history, we find a great change, in a way even a crossing of a threshold, that happened not so very long ago. To be aware of this threshold is very important to our subject.

The time of which I speak is the transition from the Egyptian culture to the Greek one. If we try to "think back" in history, back into former times, we feel ourselves more or less familiar with human civilization until we arrive at the Egyptian epoch. The Greek showed interests and activities to which we feel related, nearly acquainted. Is it not remarkable that in philosophy it is

9

often said that Greek philosophy already contained most of the elements that have been worked out since? The fact that we still learn Greek in our (European) schools is certainly significant in this respect. Also, looking at a bust of Socrates or someone else from ancient Greece, we experience someone "like us." These statues give the impression that they are looking at us! The Greeks were "here."

How different are the expressions of Egyptian pharaohs and queens! Their gaze appears to come from somewhere else, from far off in another world, as do their hieroglyphs and the *Book of the Dead.* We have no idea what lived in their soul, what they experienced in daily life, or how their language sounded. We can decipher hieroglyphs by chance—due to the discovery of the Rosetta stone—but we have no idea of how they sounded when spoken. The Egyptians were still "there." What change took place, then, in the Greek age?

I often approach this problem by asking, "Who was the first scientist to say that a fly has six legs, and why did he say so?" The answer is Aristotle, and he said it because he was interested. In this simple, even trivial example we experience the beginning of a new approach to the world of the senses. Aristotle's scientific work, which we regard as one of the greatest we possess from ancient times, can be considered as the very beginning of modern science. We can agree with this assumption better if we ask ourselves the following question. If I would like to know the difference between the chemical contents of fair hair and dark hair, I need only look it up in some book on biochemistry. Why can I find it there? The answer must be, because it has been investigated by someone. But why has he done so? The only reasonable answer is, because he was interested in it. Why are we interested? Here we do not find a solution easily. I have often asked people, "Do

you speak the Eskimo language?" Of course, hardly anyone in Europe does. When I ask, "Would you like to speak
that language?" I never find anyone who definitely says
no, or when I ask, "Do you know the meaning of the
Chinese characters?" most people agree immediately that
they certainly would like to be able to read them.

Here we meet one of the characteristics of our time:
the wish for knowledge. Knowledge, however, is closely
connected with the element of differentiation. We are interested in differentiating, but "why" is not so easy to
answer.

Here we can conclude that in the course of time came
a moment of a deep change in man's consciousness which
is manifest in his attitude toward the earth. I consider this
moment to have come in the Greek era in which Aristotle
lived and in which philosophy and thinking are supposed
to have commenced. Of course, the change began long
before.

How should we imagine such a transition of consciousness? We should not forget that we find a similar
transition in everyday human life if we study the development of our children. The glance of a child of about six or
seven months old shows an incredible fullness and even
wisdom, though no knowledge, as it is called later. This
impression is heightened if we reflect on how the smile of
such a child affects us, filling us with inexplicable feelings
of happiness. Up to his third year, the child develops a
sort of consciousness that might appear to be like ours. He
even has an incredible memory during the first three years.
The fact that later the child no longer remembers anything
of the time before the age of three can lead to only one conclusion: the child was not yet here! After his third year the
child gradually begins to develop a different, conscious
connection with his earthly environment.

In the sixteenth century the Italian philosopher, Pico della Mirandola, who wrote a wonderful essay on the dignity of man, declared, "God has created man to see Him and to love Him." If Pico della Mirandola had not been such a celebrated philosopher, he might well have been condemned to the stake for that. Nonetheless his statement is very important for our consideration; it agrees with the conception that the physical world is the exterior of a divine world, which enables man to develop a new attitude toward the spiritual world, i.e., to perceive it and to love it. Anticipating what I shall say later on the subject of belief and knowledge, I would like to emphasize that for the moment we should take these thoughts just as they are given.

The questions may then be posed: does man really recognize the divine world in his physical environment, and has humanity succeeded in coming to love that divine world? On the contrary. The word "divine" is an expression that no longer can be tolerated in scientific investigations. Furthermore, to a great extent, this "interest" in worldly phenomena—the origin of our modern attitude toward the world of the senses—has turned into an unhealthy desire. What has gone wrong?

Let us imagine, for a moment, that I discover somewhere in front of me a beautiful picture, and I think that I would like to see that picture better. I go up to it and examine it from nearby, and my admiration increases. I really would like to examine it more closely. I come nearer and nearer until I am quite close to it, and still I am not satisfied. I take a magnifying glass; I even take a microscope and come still nearer. Of course, everyone knows that in coming too close, I lose sight of the picture as a whole. The same, we could say, applies to space travel. Everyone can understand that in going to the moon we lose sight of the moon.

This has happened in the field of science. If, in the following, critical thoughts are expressed toward modern science, especially toward the field of medicine, this criticism leads back to one reproach: science has "lost sight of the world," because scientists do not keep their distance. They come too close. Man has begun to search for reality and the truth of the world by looking for details, continually more details, forgetting that truth and reality might better be found by drawing back from that same world, by surveying the part in relation to the whole. The famous Dutch anthropologist, Louis Bolk, expressed this approach in a fascinating way:

> We are in the habit of investigating life through magnifying glasses, of thus bringing otherwise invisible matter within our field of vision; how different, how much larger our concept of life would be if it were possible to study it through minimizing glasses and thus bring within our field of vision matters that are beyond the reach of the eye, taking as a goal of our studies the cohesion of the phenomena rather than the analysis of matter, as we are doing now.

This is the method we will apply to the field of medicine that we will study here: to find a new approach to the world of phenomena by gaining a proper distance through which to rediscover a reality that otherwise is lost from sight.

Knowing and Believing

The attitude of tolerance that I requested in Chapter I will not stop people from concluding, "Though I respect your conviction, I must still maintain that things not based on physical perception are a matter of belief." That is why I consider it necessary to pause for a moment at the question of the difference between knowing and believing.

I always wonder why people tend to speak in such a denigrating way about religion. I can imagine that times change, that values disappear; man is an evolving being. If, however, we wish to understand the background, the origin of religion, belief, etc., we must take into account that people in early days were different from us, different in their thinking, in their feelings, and in their occupations. Their whole relationship to the environment must have changed. The kingdoms of nature mean something totally different to us from what they did in the past. When we read that the Germanic gods, Odin and Thor, were experienced in the realm that to us belongs to the field of meteorology, or that the Greek went to the temple of Apollo to seek advice on each serious question, we should not shrug our shoulders; we should conclude that people must have been different then.

We also hear about the birth of Jesus in the beginning of our era and about the small group that formed itself around the being called Christ. What was the reason that some 300 years later Christianity had spread throughout the whole of Europe? Were those people so childish, were they so primitive, as we often tend to consider them, or should we not ask, "How was this possible?" What happened to people that they let themselves be tortured and slaughtered in the Roman arenas, let themselves be burnt at the stake during the Inquisition? Modern psychology gives, in my opinion, too easy a solution, again forgetting that it might be much more revealing to study the change of consciousness in the course of time.

This change of consciousness will, at the beginning, be our main subject. We speak about people who have their beliefs and often say that they "still" believe. I think this is appropriate, in a way. We cannot deny that the force to which we refer as belief is declining. We cannot deny that the churches are becoming increasingly empty. The aforementioned attitude of science toward belief, which creates a definite gap, is another clear example. Belief appears to be disappearing. We are not satisfied only with believing; we wish to know. Here we come to our first conclusion: when we delve back into the past, we meet an increase in the intensity and the force of belief.

Indeed, in our time we wish to know, but what does that knowing mean? We often restrict knowing to those things we can count, weigh, or measure, but these are only physical facts. There is a far more important side to knowing that is not always recognized. In reality, knowing has nothing to do with facts themselves; knowing has to do with memory. Knowing something, being sure about something, means essentially that I have the capacity for remembering it. In taking an examination, the examiner is concerned about my knowledge, which means about things I can remember. When I give testimony before a judge, to say, "I remember quite clearly" is interpreted as meaning "I know."*

In looking back some 500 years, reflecting on people to whom it meant so much to *believe* the proper thing, we come upon a similar certainty: people remembered, i.e., they *knew* what they had been told. The difference between knowledge in our time and belief in those days can be generally characterized in the following way. Knowledge is the memory leading back to the concrete, comprehensible experience that a person had some time ago. One need not have had the same experiences, however, as the scientist who did the investigations himself. In speak-

---

*If someone has no memory at all, as we may experience in people with highly developed arteriosclerosis, we say that he doesn't know anything anymore.

ing of knowledge, I would have had the same experiences that he had, had I been in the same position. If someone tells me about his travels I know that I would have seen the same things, had I been there.

In the case of belief, as considered before, things are not exactly the same. This is one of the reasons that modern man increasingly rejects belief. Belief, in the general view, has to do with tradition and dogma. What does it mean "to believe"? If someone tells me that his wallet has been stolen, I may believe him, which means that I take it for granted. Gradually belief has been restricted to this point; it means that I *accept* something to be true. Where the contents of belief originate is another question. The only thing that is more or less surprising is that the contents of belief, in connection with religions all over the world, show strong similarities. It seems a little far-fetched to claim that all these contents are merely fabricated.

If some psychologists suggest that the contents of religions are more or less invented, they are never able to indicate the moment at which this "invention" took place. They point back to some hypothetical moment, "long ago," when this must have started. We must not forget, however, that his point lies totally in the dark. Besides, as we said already, we would make a big mistake if we were to accept without discussion the supposition that man in that hypothetical time was thinking and feeling in a manner essentially similar to today.

A fruitful solution to this problem can be found if we try to picture the psychical and spiritual condition of people in very, very ancient times. We must go back in history to a point long before the transition of consciousness in the Greek age.

In both mythology and the Old Testament, we come

upon many names. These names, however, are always the name of the leaders. The people, the common folk, are never called by individual names; they appear as a group, as a unified whole. The leading figures are described as kings, priests, prophets, patriarchs, initiates, and so on. There is another expression, however, that continually appears in these tales, perhaps shedding a new light on everything. When we read names such as Agamemnon, Menelaus, Odysseus, Diomedes, we find that they are often called shepherds: ". . . and he was a shepherd to his people . . . ." This reveals something very important. In the Old Testament, too, we find many shepherds. This gives us the opportunity to form an idea about the population in ancient times; we have to do with people who were guided by shepherds. We might describe them as herds and, as the leaders are called shepherds, refer to the herds as flocks of sheep. In describing such people, whom I would like to call sheep-people, we could say that their collective appearance made them look like one another, not unlike drops of water. Whoever has seen a flock of sheep streaming over the heather, or over the pasture, or maybe has had the opportunity to see them pass through a narrow opening, will not have much difficulty comparing this image with streaming water.

We might come to the conclusion that the sheep-people in those days indeed differed little from one another; they did not lead an individual life.* They led the life of the whole group. They received group impressions, they had group feelings, and they performed group activities. This contemplation can even lead us to the con-

---

*In fact they didn't have names. It was only at the time of the Roman emperor, Augustus, that names began to be given to everybody.

clusion that they must have had a different consciousness
from ours. This consciousness can be characterized as a
"dreaming" state. Using the word "dreaming" does not
mean that they dreamt; it means that the consciousness of
the visible world did not yet have the quality that it has so
strongly for us: we "face" the world; they "underwent"
the world, as we undergo the world of our dreams, which
we can speak of as dreams only after we awake.

Can one have any idea what those dream-like perceptions were like? We are confronted with the fact that in
all mythologies we hear about gods. We are inclined to
ask how man can speak about gods when they cannot be
perceived. My answer would be that certainly *we* cannot
see gods, or let us rather say, spiritual beings, at least not
with our eyes, but who is to say that people in those days
did not see the gods with their eyes? In the Old Testament
we hear about Adam living in paradise in the midst of
divine beings. This story of Adam in paradise offers us at
the same time the possibility of lifting a tip of the veil of
this mystery. In the Old Testament, it is clearly said that
Adam did not see God with his eyes; only after Adam and
Eve were driven from paradise were their eyes opened! I
think it is important to take these words seriously, which
does not mean, of course, to take them literally. Mythological stories should be considered as pictures or images.
The organs of perception by which man was aware of his
environment created a consciousness that has been called
dream-like. Dreams can be seen as symbolic pictures.
Mythology can be considered as dreamed realities, told
by people who, in the course of history, awoke from this
dream-consciousness.

What were the organs with which Adam was able to
perceive God? It may suffice to remember that in the
whole of the Orient sense organs are still spoken of that

enabled people to perceive so-called higher worlds, the world of the creating beings. Reference to these organs is found in such expressions as Lotus-Flowers, Chakras, the third eye, etc. These are shown, for instance, in all pictures of the Buddha and other initiates as the well-known spot or knob on the forehead.

It makes sense to dwell for a moment on the expressions "gods" and "spiritual beings." We said earlier that in modern times the idea of God and similar conceptions have been rejected more and more. We should distinguish between a spiritual being in whom we believe as an almighty ruling God and the principle of a Creator. Here spiritual beings are considered to be the creating beings.

To reject the idea of a ruling almighty God suggests that man is changing his mind in such a way that he considers himself responsible for his own deeds and does not wish anyone else to be responsible for them. We have to do with a world conception in which the word god, for the moment, is being put aside. It is another question whether we can also put aside the idea of creating spiritual beings. We should recall again what we mentioned in the very beginning, that the Teutons, the Greeks, and all earlier people always spoke about spiritual beings in connection with the kingdoms of nature. The difference between our conception of nature and that of ancient people is that in those times the creating beings were still experienced, which means they were "perceived" with the help of the aforementioned supersensible organs.

We can understand a well-known expression of ancient times even better if we imagine that the awareness of the spiritual world gradually declined, became dark. The world of the gods darkened: we speak of the twilight of the gods. This includes the gradual disappearance or atrophy of the early organs of perception. The present sense organs began to predominate increasingly.

For us today there are no perceptible gods, and so we deny their existence; but if at the same time we deny the reality of creating beings, which are or were responsible for the coming into existence of the kingdoms of nature, we go too far. Modern science rejects the idea of creating beings, of the Creator in general. In the past it was said, "It is true that a watch can be constructed only by a watchmaker." Nowadays all technical forms are created by creating beings—in this case, human beings. It is supposed, however, that forms in nature came into existence by chance, not by creation; in other words, without a "watchmaker." I do not think it is reasonable to discuss the problem of the watchmaker *in extenso*. Even if I do not know who the watchmaker is, even if I am unable to perceive the creating beings, I need not deny their existence. When I consider plant, animal, and man as creations, it is not an arbitrary hypothesis; I am not inventing something out of the blue. I recognize the form as a creation.

I "recognize" it means nothing more than that I know quite well what creation is, because I am a creator myself. The question of what the creating beings are and where they are to be found, perceived, or approached is something else. The essential point is that modern science rejects the idea of creating beings in nature partly because our feeling for reality depends on physical appearances. If ever the reality of spiritual beings is to be acknowledged, we must educate our way of relating to them in such a way that it satisfies our modern feeling for reality.

We can conclude for the moment that the contents of belief of which we have spoken already may be brought into relation to experiences, perceptions, and awarenesses that no longer exist for us today but that may well have been present in the distant past. There is, however, another consideration that brings us back to the issue of knowledge and memory. Our memory is either poor or rich in experiences, depending on the way we have lived, on the life we have led, and on our capacity for remembering. Our knowledge—the content of all our memories—is thus very personal. Each of us carries a totally different memory within. On the average, this memory-picture shows a clearly arranged, distinct, inner world in which we can even distinguish some spatial element, an expression of extension, along with an element of time expressed in words such as recently, long ago, etc. Not everyone has the same number of memories, of course, and indeed, few memories go back beyond the third year. If someone is asked his age, he can give two answers: the age indicated in his passport, or the length of his memory, which generally will be three years less. To grow old means to gain a longer past, and we thus can say that a person is as old as his or her memory.

What about the people we just mentioned, the "sheep-people"? We may accept that they also had experiences that they remembered. As their experiences were group experiences, we may call their memory a group memory. What they experienced and what they remembered must in those days have been uniform for the group.

Let us consider for a moment how memories come into existence. The only possibility is that the impressions we receive from our senses, which are the source of our experiences, create some sort of "imprint" on our constitution. We need not bother about where these impressions are located. The main point is that we distinguish clearly between an impression made on us in the psychical sense of the word and the impression that has been imprinted somewhere on our body. In remembering this impression, it becomes again a part or element of my soul life; it is "remembered." The body in which the impressions are made is, we should not forget, a living body.

This creates an unexpected point of view; e.g., it stands to reason that the impressions that were made on the body could have participated in the laws of heredity. The form of our body was inherited; so too were the impressions that settled in our living body as forms. We thus could come to an understanding that experiences, as part of our memories, were inheritable. Imagine for a moment that a son inherited a body that bore the general qualities of race, tribe, family, etc., along with impressions that had been imprinted in the constitution by experiences which in that sense were "rememberable." We know quite well that there is no question of any similar experience in our time. We should not forget, however, that, speaking about the past, we have to do with a uniform group humanity. This means nothing less than that a son was able to remember the experiences of his father. As the father had been in the same situation, however, the son eventually might be able to remember even the experiences of his grandfather, his great-grandfather, and so on. People did not experience themselves as individuals; they did not really have an individual soul life. They led the life of the group; we may thus speak about group-souls.

What was the consequence? People had very long memories, stretching far back into the past. Following the formula that man is as old as his memory, we might conclude that man grew incredibly old, as he looked into a past that reached back hundreds of years. The information that people grew as old as is told us in the Old Testament, sometimes even lived well over 900 years (Methuselah), becomes clear to us now. This also enlightens us about the fact that we so often come upon the same name in the course of different generations. We hear about several Zarathustras in the Persian time. We might even say the same name referred to everyone belonging to that same family or generation. People identified themselves more or less with the person who stood at the beginning. The well-known expression, "I and Father Abraham are one" offers another example. Of course, we have to do with the leaders as representatives of their people, who also participated in the group memory. Even later, much later, people had the habit of calling themselves the sons of their fathers. A person would call himself son of John, son of Peter, etc. This changed into John's son, Peter's son; we thus find the origin of the names Johnson, Peterson. The main point of these considerations, however, is how man's consciousness has changed in the course of time.

The memory of earlier people was a very long one and reached far into the past. It expressed what people knew, but what they knew were experiences also of long, long ago, of times in which humanity perhaps had an awareness of worlds and spiritual beings through organs of perception that later disappeared. We may conclude that what people knew then was based on experiences.

Why do we not have such experiences today? Our memory has become short and, at the same time, personal. The strong light of our consciousness, which we may refer to as "awake" in contrast to the old "dreaming" consciousness, pushes back, so to speak, everything that could be realized only under the conditions of the past. This is also the reason that conscious memories are no longer inheritable. It enables us, however, also to approach the problem of belief with a very delicate question. Could it be that the divine experiences were a reality in the past, just as our individual experiences were a reality in our past? What we call believing is a remnant of knowing in the past, in which people had experiences that we no longer have. Because they were real experiences of a divine world, however, they still convey to us that peculiar and often impressive light that is attributed by so many people to the field of belief.

The foregoing has been brought up in connection with the words belief, divine, and religion. The beginnings of Christianity lie much later, when we must deal with a consciousness in humanity that is more related to our own. To establish a link between the happenings in the beginning of our era, in Palestine, and to our time, we must find, we must discover, a new and different approach. This discovery will be one of the major aims of the following sections.

A Characteristic of Medicine in the Beginning of the Twentieth Century

When, in the early 1920's, we were given our first clinical lessons, our professor addressed us, saying, "Ladies and gentlemen, when the diagnosis has been made, the doctor has done his duty." In Dutch everyday language, he even expressed this as, "For the doctor, the fun is over." What he meant to say was that there was no therapy, so to speak.

From an Austrian friend I learned that even in the beginning of the 1930s a similar view and attitude existed among the medical faculty at the University of Vienna. The professor would discuss, in a very sophisticated manner, the development of the diagnosis and then leave the room, leaving his students and some of his assistants to puzzle over the problem of some therapeutic treatment.

Of course, even in 1920 there existed a certain number of traditional prescriptions. Digitalis (in the form of pulvis folio digitalis—the crumbled leaves), quinine, strophantus and its derivatives, opium, bromium, and so on, as well as a few chemical compounds such as salversan and aspirin, had already appeared on the market. On the whole, however, the attitude toward medication was as I just described. This attitude, as a concept, is called nihilism. Nihilism lived in the minds of those in the medical world in the nineteenth century. In certain ways it even became appropriate for a doctor to be a nihilist. Doctors went around, made diagnoses and prognoses, and their main treatment consisted of venesection (bloodletting) and the prescription of purgatives. Ricinus oil and castor oil stood in high favor!

This somewhat astonishing description of the situation in the nineteenth century will be discussed much more elaborately later. For the moment, however, it is necessary to describe two phenomena that accompanied the above-mentioned attitude of nihilism. The first is best expressed in what I have often experienced as a certain attitude of modesty. "We can do nothing," doctors repeated in meetings or gatherings. A second very important phenomenon was that illness, to a certain degree, was accepted as part of human life. One had to accept the fact that illness existed. A certain fatalism was felt.

Since that time much has changed, particularly since the second World War and starting already at the end of the 1930s. One who is acquainted with the incredible number of new medicines that have gradually appeared —insulin (against diabetes), Permaemon (later Vitamin B12, against pernicious anaemia), the antibiotics, the tranquillizers and psychofarmica, the anticoagulants (against thrombosis), cortisone (think of all rheumatic illnesses), the extensive use of estrogens, sleeping tablets, pain killers, which are showing unexpected and surprising effects—will not be astonished at encountering a totally new situation. The previous feeling of modesty has vanished and been replaced by the conviction that it is only a matter of time before every illness can be healed. Should we wonder that a certain pride has taken the place of modesty?

The change in attitude towards illness as such is terribly important in this regard. Instead of recognizing illness as part of human life, the belief has grown increasingly that "illness should not be." To put it in this way probably shows best the fundamental change in attitude. This attitude characterizes the modern medical world presiding over our time. Those who think differently are, if accepted at all, given the label "alternative." It would be difficult to discuss the question with modern medical scientists of whether perhaps *they* are alternative. Nobody need be angry or offended at this suggestion. I only intend to characterize the situation in which we find ourselves today. Modern allopathic medicine, accepted as *the* medicine, was established in the course of a long, long development, going back to what we call the origin of modern treatment, back to the time of the great Hippocrates, who began to develop the trend of thinking that predominates today. This is the general conception. With Hippocrates, therefore, modern medicine finds its point of origin. Ever since, knowledge has increased slowly, step by step, until it has gathered the vast number of scientific facts in our possession today. We have just shown, however, that this is not true in every respect. Our modern medicine is incredibly young, not much more than fifty years old. As we stated earlier, in the nineteenth century nihilism was the general attitude.

When we speak of the time of Hippocrates as a starting point) is it not logical, then, to expect that from that time on we should encounter an increase in medical knowledge and also advances in the field of healing? We know how great the increase in anatomical and physiological knowledge has been, but what about the problem of healing?

How did man feel about healing in the time of Hippocrates? Were the primitive doctors filled with feelings of nihilism? I do not think so. We will try to develop here a new understanding of the history of medicine, healing included. The first question that will arise is, though Hippocrates is considered the founder of modern medicine, what existed before Hippocrates? What do we know about even older times?

Before continuing I must warn against a possible error. So often in medical history we meet this concept: "There were certainly methods of treatment well before Hippocrates. Some traditions have come down to us, but we don't think it important to consider these very primitive methods. They are of hardly any value to us." This is a great mistake indeed! That is why I must elaborate on the concept of the "primitiveness" of ancient times.

III

The History of Medicine

Egypt: Healing in Early Times

We will have to determine first of all our method of investigation. If we are mainly discussing the question of what people did, of what the nature of the treatments was in ancient times, we are too one-sided. It is not only the treatments themselves that we must study but the people also—what were they like? If we continue to assume that people in those days were primitive, knowing little *but otherwise possessing the same consciousness that we have,* struck by the same illnesses for which diagnoses had not been worked out in a distinct way, then further discussion will be senseless. These assumptions show so much prejudice that it would be difficult to draw attention to a new approach.

To what extent, then, was primitive man primitive? By contemplating only the results of our technology, we might easily overlook the essentials. Have we ever asked ourselves how life on earth, before technology came into being, was established? It is true, technology has achieved an incredible height of perfection and still continues to do so. If we consider primitive man as we generally do, however, as a half-naked ape-man with a cudgel in his hand, dragging a wife behind him—as we

29

often see in pictures in which the artist has truly followed
the concept that man is an evolved ape—we cannot imagine how such a wild-looking being could have managed
to cultivate plants with which to feed himself, breed cat-
tle, discover and forge metals, or develop the science of
mathematics at which we marvel (the Aztecs, etc.).*

Louis Bolk, the renowned anthropologist, said he considered the person who invented the first plow to have
been a greater genius than any inventor today. I do not
think it difficult to feel his point. His words are,

> The first chapter on the evolution of the human spirit will
> have to begin with the words 'In the beginning was the
> genius.' He who first came upon the idea of composing a
> plow in its most primitive form topped all inventors of
> later times, for whom posterity has erected so many
> statues.**

These thoughts fully accord with the ideas we
developed earlier concerning humanity in the past.
Returning once more to the situation in those days, we
find a group consciousness among the people who were
guided by the initiate-kings. We could express this in the
following manner: the people clung to the king, the kings
clung to heaven. We thus can understand how these kings
were able to develop a wisdom far beyond the capacity of
what man on earth could have developed in the way we
do now. We could call the source of their knowledge "inspiration." Such an experience (and expression) still exists, though in a different form, today. What does "inspiration" mean here? It indicates the aforementioned

---

*In response to Desmond Morris's *The Naked Ape*, another interpretation is offered in my book, *The Dressed Angel*, Regency Press, London, New York,
1975.
**L. Bolk, *Brain and Culture*, 1918.

connection that existed in consciousness between man and the creating beings in nature.

Here I can give a clear example. One of the tasks of the old kings was to cultivate the earth, as has already been mentioned. What does this mean? Nothing less, in those times, than the cultivation of wheat from grass! We should marvel greatly at such a capacity in epochs generally labeled as "primitive"! How could a king, an initiate, know how to grow wheat from grass? The answer could be, "By asking the grass." If we, in modern times, try to cultivate new varieties of some sort of flower, we must do experiments, but what does that mean, to do experiments? It means to test the laws that eventually dictate the result! It is in a certain way a questioning without words!

In ancient times there was no experimentation, but for our modern consciousness, modern science is necessary. The ancient kings were able to question not the grass-plant itself, of course, but the being responsible for the creation of it! This means that the initiates were able to contact the creating world in a spiritual way. It is of great importance for what follows to understand this conclusion; it enables us to comprehend the way in which in earlier days the knowledge of herbs was established. The specific quality of herbs was experienced by what we could call direct inspiration from the divine world. Humanity was still directed toward the periphery, toward the cosmos. We will soon see how fruitful this idea is for understanding what we know as "medical treatment" in Egyptian times, for we know hardly anything at all about still older times.

In looking at treatment in Egyptian times we come upon the phrase "temple sleep." I would like to quote Paul Hühnerfeld from his book on the history of medicine: "Nowadays it is difficult to judge what the healing force of the temple sleep may have been."* I will try to show how we may have to change our way of thinking to deal with this problem in the most comprehensive way. To begin, we might ask, what is sleep? In spite of the efforts of modern physiology that often complicate the problem, I think that the answer to this question is not so difficult. To fall asleep means to leave; to wake up means to. enter.** He who falls asleep leaves his body; he who wakes up enters his body again. "He" includes you and me, refering to the being who says "I" to himself. This information is not difficult to accept if only we do away with prejudices that have been created so extensively during the last centuries. We cannot say that at any point in history man ever invented the idea that he was a being, a spiritual being, a reality in itself. On the contrary, man never invented anything like that idea; this understanding was a matter of course, it was an immediate experience of daily life that has never disappeared but that has been concealed by the prejudices of modern physiology. It is not so long ago that words like "soul" and "spirit" were utter realities to everyone. In the course of the last centuries, however, these concepts gradually have been abolished. Later we will see that the same happened with the idea of "life" as a reality in itself.

We may ask, what prevents us from sleeping? Insomnia is a common complaint nowadays. The answer can be

---

*Paul Hühnerfeld, *Kleine Geschichte der Medizin*. Signum, Gutersloh.

**We need not worry about the biochemical changes that take place in our body. As will become clear later, these changes should not be considered the cause but the consequence of "falling asleep." It may even be interesting to consider that taking a sleeping drug never causes a normal sleep; it only prevents us from remaining awake. We are, so to speak, "kicked" out of our body (which may, however, sometimes be welcome).

quite short: something prevents us from leaving the body, something keeps us within it. The cause of this problem is to be found either in the body itself (physical ailment, pains) or in the soul (psychological problems, worries).

Comparing the life of an ancient Egyptian to a modern European, we may presume that sleep was certainly a different experience for earlier people with a group consciousness. Out of what has been said about ancient and modern consciousness, we may conclude that in those days the distance between being awake and being asleep was less wide.

Let us consider "temple sleep." This must have been a special sort of sleep. Sleep as such can have only two qualities: superficial and deep. If people in those days generally slept well, we can take it that temple sleep was a deeper sleep than normal. This assumption allows us to approach the significance of temple sleep in a surprising way. For this purpose, however, I should like to make a small, instructive, if not amusing, detour. A husband leaves his house in the morning to go to his office. In the evening he returns. Let us imagine that his wife is glad to have him return. In any case, once a year it may happen that the wife asks her husband, "When you leave the house this morning, will you do me a favor and stay away for a whole week?" Why, what is the matter? I am speaking of the time of spring cleaning, and in the same way I imagine that temple sleep means a much deeper sleep than a normal one, for the sake of a similar sort of event. Instead of cleaning, however, we might speak of healing. In the temple sleep man left his body so that other beings could enter it and do their healing work. Which beings? I do not consider it a problem to find the appropriate answer. Something had to be restored. What had to be restored? The human body, the human form. Who should

be able to accomplish the restoration? The being, or beings, that had created that form in the first place. They
carried the real possibility of restoring the "cover" in
which man lives when he is awake; they could "recover."

Let us recall what has been said until now and try to
imagine how things happened in practice. One can imagine that people suffering from psychical or physical
symptoms were brought to the temple by the priest to
undergo a temple sleep as a process of healing. The
recuperation took place during the sleep; the priest could
consciously guide the spiritual beings in their restoring
activities. We might come to a very delicate conclusion:
here we have a wonderful example of what healing
means in reality. Someone guides the healing forces into
the "deformed" body! What was the result of the annihilation of the deformation or deterioration of the
form? The result was that man could continue his
development, continue his "way."

We need not think that healing through temple sleep
was the only healing activity in those days. It is certain
that herbs were used and other substances of nature.
Baths were also given. However, our information is poor.
At the same time, we must never forget that people approached springs, plants, and mineral substances very
differently from the way we do. We may remind ourselves of what has been said about the impressions that
people in those days had of the kingdoms of nature.
Nature was also the result of the activity of the creating
beings, with whom special people in those days could
come into relationship. Because of that, they were able to
know the connection between herbs and illness. This
knowledge has disappeared in modern science.

In any case, a special remark must be made in view of
the fact that modern man will generally shrug his

shoulders when he hears about healing through temple sleep; he will think it hardly worth considering. Let us not forget, however, that this treatment was used for thousands of years! To me, the only sensible attitude toward the phenomenon of healing through temple sleep is to admit that we do not know about the nature of the ailments that it healed. The only thing we do know is that the treatment was apparently effective for a long period, and one night could be sufficient for the healing.

We must therefore be very careful to consider the nature of the ailment as such. It is not easy to give an exact picture. We know of only a few illnesses that existed in ancient days, if we exclude wounds. It is true that some information has been gathered in the examination of mummies, and the conclusion has been arrived at that people in those days suffered from the same illnesses from which we suffer nowadays. Here lies a pitfall, however. This idea has only been built up by interpreting some phenomena in a very special way. It is a matter of interpretation of facts. Even in light of these facts, we cannot ignore the change in the human being over the ages. We will return to this subject later.

What can we imagine about illnesses that were healed in one night during a temple sleep? What sort of illness can be restored in so short a time? The illnesses must have been common to many people, not, for example, osteomyelitis and diabetes, which are believed to have existed already in those days and which, of course, could never be healed in a single night! The only expression that seems to cover the illnesses healed through temple sleep is the general term "deformation" of the form. Needless to say, we must imagine these deformations to have been of different character. This is already illustrated by the fact that plants and other substances apparently were used also, which suggests a longer treatment. How these treatments can be understood will be explained in the section, "The Practice of Healing."

What was the cause of this deformation? Here we may introduce something that already has its parallel in modern times. We have spoken about a deformation. A deformation of the human form is, in some way, always a deterioration. Let us not hesitate to consider something that once happened in human evolution, something called the fall of man into matter. Here we touch upon the principle of sinning. Throughout the history of medicine we come upon the advice of doctors to patients to change their way of life. I think it advantageous to put two and two together: the cause of the deformation was sought in the soul life. In modern times, in the last thirty or forty years, a new field of medicine has been developed: psychosomatic medicine, in which human behavior, character, and so forth are thought to influence health and constitution. To me it is easy to recognize a link between these modern discoveries and "sin" and "deformation" in the Egyptian era. Later we will find a comprehensible solution to this problem; for the moment, we leave the question open as to the nature of the deformation with which we are dealing. As to the problem of characterizing the people in Egyptian times as a whole, we will limit ourselves to the expression: humanity was highly connected with the gods.

Treatment	Illness	Humanity
	Egypt	
Temple sleep----------- Deformation (?)--- Connected with the gods		
Prayers		
Herbs		

Greece: Medicine Before Hippocrates

Now we come to the early Greek period. Here we find a new situation in the three realms we are going to contemplate: treatment, illness, and humanity. We consider this transition to have taken place at the time of Hippocrates. We have to understand that during the Greek era medicine must be divided into two distinct periods: the time before and the time after Hippocrates.

We have already elaborated on the great change that took place in human consciousness during the Greek period. Man developed the capacity of thinking. It is of the greatest importance to understand that the moment man began to think, his consciousness underwent a deep change. We are, all of us, thinking beings; everyone knows that he thinks and in spite of the difficulty of giving a definition of thinking, everyone knows what it means. Through thinking, the human being developed a new way of understanding his environment and also his fellow man. Such a development began only in the Greek period. This is the reason we experience such an affinity between Greek times and modern times, as we suggested already in Chapter II.

We must speak first about the development of medicine during the first half of the Greek era. The term temple sleep gives way to the phrase temple dream. We have descriptions about Epidaurus from which we become acquainted with what people relate after having experienced a temple dream treatment; they recount their dreams. These dreams almost always contained the vision of a god whom they saw, who spoke to them, who promised to heal them under special conditions—mainly making offerings and worshipping—and after waking they found themselves healed. Of course in our time, many of us will listen to these stories with certain reservations. When we put them next to the account we have given of the Egyptian times, however, the matter becomes less improbable. We can feel the increase in consciousness—from sleeping to dreaming.

Just as the temple sleep in the Egyptian times was conducted by a priest, so too the priest conducted, so to speak, the dreaming activity of the sick person in the Greek period. On waking the patient had to tell his dream. We have adequate information about these dreams. Among the ruins of the temple of Epidaurus, archeologists have found so-called "stiles" (engraved stone tablets); on them are written in the Doric language the names of the patients who were healed by Asclepius, as well as their illnesses. The cases of which we have information are not very specific. They often give the impression of being symbolic pictures, in a certain way. We will give some examples:

A man, who could move only one finger, came to the god (to the temple), asking for help. When he entered the sanctuary, he observed many flat stones on which stories of healings were engraved. He laughed at them and could not believe that they were true. He even mocked them. As he fell asleep in the temple afterward, he had a vision. He dreamt that he was playing dice under the temple and that the god appeared and jumped on his hand. The god stretched his fingers and told him to try out the flexibility. He was able to stretch all his fingers in the normal way. The god then asked him whether he now believed the stories carved in the holy stones; the man said, "Yes." "Because you were unbelieving before, though the stories were not unbelievable, your name will in the future be 'non-believer.' " The next morning he left the temple in good health.

There was also one-eyed Ambrosia from Athens. The moment she entered the sanctuary, she laughed at the pretended former healings and could not believe that paralyzed and blind people were healed just by having seen a dream. After she had fallen asleep in the "dormitorium," she had a vision: she dreamt that a god approached her and told her that she would be healed on the condition that she would sacrifice a silver swine in memory of her ignorance. After having said she would do so, he cut open her blind eye and poured some medicine into it. In the morning she left the temple healed.

Of course these are extreme examples, but for the most part we encounter some form of paralysis, blindness, muteness, and in some cases we come across the healing of wounds caused by war. We are certainly not confronted with illnesses with which we are acquainted. An exception, no doubt, is the case of someone suffering from a "stone." We may even have to do with a kidney stone, which in our days we consider to be caused by a disturbance of the biochemistry in the bladder; we could call it a functional deformation. One of the stories tells us of a little boy, who dreamt that the god asked him, "What will you offer me when I deliver you of your stone?" The boy said, "Ten marbles." The god smiled, and in the morning the child was healed.

Two things should be emphasized here. First of all, people were requested by the god to sacrifice something. In addition, only those could be healed who believed. We must keep these two points in mind for future reference.

I should like to describe a remarkable experience encountered in medical practice today. In an article in a Dutch magazine, *Arts en Wereld* (Physician and World), May 1978, a Dutch doctor, Tine Kaayk, mentions the following about one of her patients.:

She was an amiable, middle-aged lady when she came under my treatment. She often came to me with abdominal complaints caused by a chronic appendicitis from which she suffered greatly. As she had serious heart trouble, an operation was out of the question. She accepted this and adapted herself to a very quiet life. Each visit we had a pleasant talk. She was acquainted with many subjects relating to spiritual life, and I remember having had many agreeable conversations with her. One year, after a holiday, visiting her again, she looked quite well and told me, full of enthusiasm, that her appendix had been taken out. Apparently this had not caused any problem at all, so I concluded that I had been overcautious. When I asked who had operated and in what clinic, she told me it had been performed in her own home in her own bed! After a day of much pain, she found herself in a condition between waking and sleeping in the evening and had the impression that a couple of doctors in white overalls were gathering around her bed; she felt something happening in her abdomen. It did not really hurt, but she had the impression of some pulling. Afterward, she fell asleep and never had pain anymore. Twelve years later she died, free of any complaints. What happened here? Does anyone know about similar experiences?

We have spoken about healing through spiritual beings during the temple sleep of the Egyptian times. If we understand that in the Greek era the same healings occurred, though now the patients had an awareness of what happened and therefore dreamt of those beings in manifold ways, the story mentioned above becomes comprehensible. It is true that we live in the twentieth century, but we have heard that the lady had a great interest in questions of the spirit, so she must have been sensitive to some extent to spiritual impressions. We should not forget, however, that many people know of dreams that clearly picture sensations accompanying physical troubles. This lady's dream can well be regarded as a wonderful illustration of what eventually healing always is: restoration of the form. The lady really had a very special experience of what, in reality, may lie behind every healing process in the human body.

In the Greek period, unlike in the Egyptian epoch, we meet individualities who are known historically. I would like to mention just four of them: Pythagoras, Empedocles, Democrates of Abdera, and Diogenes of Apollonia. We need not go into details about their activities, but in order to arrive at a good understanding it is necessary to offer a brief impression of them. We all know the name of Pythagoras, in connection with his theorem. Pythagoras was a mathematician and a musician. He concerned himself with the question of harmony and disharmony, equilibrium and disequilibrium. To him, man stems from what is called "the harmony of the spheres." Illness to him was, to some extent, a problem of disharmony between the spiritual and the earthly elements of man. What was before an instinctive understanding regarding illness becomes a comprehensible thought. Empedocles spoke about composition and decomposition of the right relationship between the four elements: earth, water, air, and warmth. In line with Pythagoras' formulation, Empedocles used the expression, right or wrong "mixture." The right mixture he called love, the wrong mixture he called hatred. Both Pythagoras and Empedocles treated those who were ill by regulating their way of life so as to change a disorder into harmony.

Democrates was the first to speak of the atom. He considered man to be an atomic spiral, spiraling in and out, in birth and death, but also in illness and in health. Diogenes saw the essence of illness and healing in the realm of respiration, the air, in the *"pneuma."* Air was life. Again, in both cases we find the rhythm of connection and disconnection. In all four examples we see that conceptions at that time still related to those in the Egyptian period. A strong awareness of the divine still lived in the human soul.

This connection with the divine, also evident in temple healing, is underlined by the fact that the Greek used to consider the origin of medical art to be connected with a particular god: Asclepius. It is a well-known fact that in the time of Hippocrates and even later, wealthy Greeks who were healed of an illness used to offer a rooster as a sacrifice to the god. Even Socrates, before dying, reminded his friends: "Don't forget to offer a rooster to Asclepius."

Hippocrates—a Threshold

When we come to Hippocrates, who is considered the initiator of modern medicine, we may ask what his "specialty" was. What made him different from his predecessors? What was the original element he added to medical knowledge? It is the way he started to write down and describe the phenomena of illness. He was the first to make classifications, to develop what is called diagnoses. His conception of the origin of illness was that health should be a balanced mixture of the four elements in man: black gall, yellow gall, phlegm, and blood; illness indicated an incorrect mixture. Many of us will wonder what he meant thereby. I wonder whether we will ever quite understand, but of one thing we can be sure: it reminds us in some way of the four elements—earth, water, air, warmth—which constituted the human body, as we have seen, in the conception of Empedocles.*

---

*We are even reminded of the four kingdoms—mineral, plant, animal and man—in which the four elements appear in about the same order.

In order to find our way into the meaning behind say-
ings and expressions from Empedocles, Hippocrates,
Democrates, and Diogenes, I would like to say the
following. When Empedocles speaks about earth, water,
air, and warmth, one might think that he, for the first
time, began to discriminate between the four elements.
When we think also of the four liquids of Hippocrates,
however, and at the same time do not forget how human
consciousness was closely connected with the wisdom in
nature, we are reminded of the fact that leading people in
those days visited mystery schools, of which it was forbid-
den, by penalty of death, to reveal anything. The story of
Aeschylus is well known; he was condemned to death
because he was accused of betraying mystery secrets. He
was saved only by the fact that he could prove that he
never actually had been initiated in a mystery school. The
thought that the words of Empedocles, Hippocrates,
Democrates, and Diogenes contain many symbolic mean-
ings begins, I believe, to reveal more. We should not take
them as words with the same meaning as that to which
we are accustomed in modern times.

We must consider these personalities as initiates. In
those early times healing was the task of the mystery
schools, just as later for many centuries, healing was
mainly the task of the convents. It is as if some old knowledge is still working into the thinking and feeling of Hippocrates and that this meets with a new consciousness
and method regarding medicine, which has since pro-
vided the basis of our modern medical knowledge.

Let us linger for a moment on these words. Some ancient knowledge still penetrates the thinking and feeling
of Hippocrates. The fact that the institution of modern
medicine leads back to Hippocrates shows that he is considered as representing a turning point in medical history,
which is not the same as a starting point! Here we will

build up a picture of the personality of Hippocrates, first of all by considering his name. What does "Hippocrates" mean? It means someone who "reins horses" (*Hippos* = horse, *kratein* = to rein). This reminds us of many cases in Greek history and in mythological history—we touched upon this in the beginning—in which we meet the same names. We hear about Hipponoös ("he who knows the horse"), Hippodameia ("she who tames the horse"), Hippolochos ("he who lays in wait for the horse"), Hippothoös ("he who is like a running horse"), and so on.

To solve this riddle we must ask what was hidden in the image of the horse in ancient times. It is helpful to remember the story of Cheiron, a demi-god, half man, half horse, who was the wise teacher of so many other demi-gods. Cheiron himself recounted his development to his pupil, Heracles, saying that once he had been a wild, lawless, destroying being, a centaur. He then continued, "Once we were chased by Apollo. I fell and broke my leg, but Apollo didn't kill me; he healed me. Pallas Athene taught me; my fire was not extinguished but became mild, and so I became what I am now."

Cheiron was known to be the wisest being on earth. How can we relate this to what he revealed about himself? Here we must accept an old conception that viewed the horse as the epitome of the whole animal kingdom. Animals are not only the often aggressive and always desireful beings that we generally take them to be. We should not forget that an animal is a being with a marvelous knowledge, albeit an inborn knowledge, which we call instinct. If we think of a spider and the incredible "wisdom" that lives in its ability to weave its web with ever-so-many threads, which are excreted from ever-so-many glandular openings, we can only marvel. A being that possessed the inborn wisdom of all animals had to be an incredibly wise being; but this wisdom can reveal itself as wisdom only if the animal knowledge is transformed into human knowledge. We may quote a wonderful saying from Teilhard de Chardin, who characterized the difference between animal and man as follows: "The animal knows; man is the only being who knows that he knows." Here we can recognize Cheiron's story: the moment his human half mastered the animal half, he came into possession of the greatest cosmic wisdom.* We may conclude that the horse was the image of total cosmic wisdom, which means the wisdom we can recognize in nature-revelations.** Hence, those names we find in mythology that begin with "*hippo*" were given to many demi-gods, kings, and shepherds in ancient times.

In speaking of Hippocrates as a personality at the end of one epoch and at the beginning of another, we may now understand better the significance of his name. On the one hand, he still bore the past; on the other hand, he introduced the future. A feeling of reverence can rise in our souls when we think of the important role played by individualities like Hippocrates. Medicine at the time of

---

*Another very attractive example is that of Hipponoös. He was the grandson of Sisyphus and of great beauty and intelligence. During the time of his trials he was given the task of fighting the chimera, a sphinx-like monster that destroyed the fields and attacked women, children, and travelers. To help him in achieving his task, the gods gave him a white, winged horse, Pegasus, on which he was able to lift himself into the air and so manage to kill the beast. Again we have to do with a picture that shows a human being, not part horse, as Cheiron was, but mastering a winged horse; the animal wisdom is brought aloft to the human level.

**All that man discovers as knowledge about *qualities* in the mineral world, *forms* in plant life, and *intelligence* in animal instincts may be seen as revelations. This wisdom is concealed: Man strives to discover it in his scientific studies.

Hippocrates still revealed early conceptions that sound strange to us today but that kept their strength for many centuries.

Should we not ask at what moment in his life Hippocrates was given his name? Were the names of Plato, Empedocles, and Pythagoras given to them from birth? If not, who gave them their special names and at which moment in their lives were they given? It was only after an initiation that a person was given his special name. We might also put it this way: the mystery-name was given by the hierophant* at the moment the particular individual was considered worthy of the name. We thus gain even more understanding of the past.**

---

*High priest.

**I cannot prevent myself from giving a last example of a connection of the expression *"hippos"* with ancient, cosmic wisdom. It is the word "hippodrome." Hippodrome means race track, as well as circus, but in great Greek tragedies it is also used for the orbit of the sun! Helios was supposed to follow the sun-orbit with a cart drawn by horses. Let us imagine how being connected with horse wisdom leads back to being connected with sun wisdom, or cosmic wisdom. Again we find the cosmic element in the word, in the image of the horse.

What is a circus and what happens in a circus? A circus must be round. I think that is compulsory. You cannot have a circus in a square space. A circus has a vault; a flat roof is unthinkable. What is the real character of performances in a circus? Certainly, it is totally different from performances on the stage. I would even like to limit real circus work to six examples: trapeze, juggling, tightrope walking, clowns, trained horses, and animal-taming. Trapeze: swinging through the air high in the vault; juggling: bringing earthly objects into unearthly conditions; tightrope walking: freeing oneself from the earth; clowns: not taking events on earth seriously; trained horses: mounted on horseback as the horse slows into a walk, the rider swings along the circumference of a figure eight, a lemniscate, from right, then over the left, right forward and left backward, and so forth, the image of a planetary orbit! Animal-taming: the image of Cheiron! To me the atmosphere in a circus is something other than the earthly. There is something extraordinary, which may be regarded as a last remnant of realities that could be approached only by a different consciousness.

It could be that in our day humanity is beginning to tire of being separated

Asking ourselves about the nature of illnesses in the Greek era, as we did regarding the Egyptian age, we meet similar problems. When we are confronted with the diagnoses of Hippocrates, we look to understand what Hippocrates really meant. We should not suppose that he was already making the same clear distinctions we find in our modern approach. Often it is stated that Hippocrates was acquainted with malaria. There may be some truth in this statement, but we must call to mind for a moment what we know about malaria. Malaria is an infection caused by a parasite called Plasmodium Vivax, which is passed on to us by a mosquito, called Anopheles Maculipennis. The Plasmodium Vivax penetrates our red blood corpuscles, multiplies, and builds special daisy-like forms. These are but few facts from an elaborate, modern-day description of malaria.

At the time of Hippocrates the picture was considerably different. Malaria was an illness caused by unhealthy surroundings, particularly moors. It was the air that was the cause of the disease bad air, *mal aria,* as is indicated in the Latin phrase. We can sense the great difference between these diagnoses, in spite of the fact that the word is the same, but were the symptoms of the illness then identical with those of our time?

from the higher worlds. We live in a time of definite materialism, which has become an ideal in many realms of science, an ideal that was expressed first by Du Bois-Reymond and Brücke in 1842. They promised one another to accept as a general law that each phenomenon in nature and on earth be explained by purely physical facts.

This point of view has certainly contributed a great deal to the incredible results of modern science and technology. Another question is whether man as a spiritual being can at length live with these conceptions. Maybe humanity is beginning to tire of the rejection of every thought, every argument that points to different realities from those determined by modern science as the only acceptable ones. Maybe a first ray of light lives in many a young person as a longing for conscious reconciliation. Is that the reason young people often used to call themselves "hippies"?

We find something similar in the case of rheumatism; this word, translated literally, stems from *rheo*, meaning flowing; rheumatic complaints thus can be conceived as blockages in something that flowed. It has been spoken of as floating pains, and perhaps we can recognize what the experiences are in the case of "rheumatic pain" in a shoulder, in a muscle, in a nerve, to give only simple examples. We can find another approach to the expression "rheumatic," however. We experience the effect of troubles in our limbs and connected parts of our body especially in our movements. The normally "streaming movements" are checked, inhibited; we have a rheumatic problem. It is difficult to detect the real significance of the word "rheumatism" used for an illness, but we should by no means think that the elaborate conceptions we have developed about rheumatism as a whole can be compared to the ideas of Hippocrates.

What were the treatments Hippocrates used? We may assume that the temple dream treatment had not entirely vanished. Plants and herbs were used widely, but we do not know much about them, and we should not forget the description of how a plant was found, how a healer, priest, or doctor discovered the plant; it was certainly not by investigations that bear any resemblance to our own methods. Apart from herbs, prescriptions were given in the form of diets, baths, especially in spring-wells, and an attention to one's way of life. Man had to master his exuberances. It is interesting that we nearly always hear of illnesses at that time caused by an excess, by "too much," rarely by "too little."

A final treatment of particular interest to our investigation is the laying on of hands; today we would speak of magnetism and label it as an "alternative treatment." In those days many people practiced such an art, and they were greatly respected. Again we must understand that such a treatment must be looked at differently, depending on the qualities of the person who performs it and of the person who receives it. One word may suffice to explain what I mean. Humanity, on the whole, was more "open" at that time. He was not so separated from his "environment" as we are today. When we are confronted with treatment by magnetism today, we still hear about outstreaming from the hands. Though we may consider this treatment obsolete, we should not forget how much circumstances and constitutions have changed. This may also be the reason that modern medical treatment is making less and less use of bathing cures. The effect of these cures—taking therapeutic baths—may indeed have grown less impressive. This could, however, quite well be due to the fact that the human body is much more shut off from its environment than it used to be in early times.

If we ask ourselves what humanity was like during the Greek epoch compared with the preceding Egyptian times, we find certain differences. The main point is that we no longer speak of a group-people, as we did previously. The human being has become more individualized, and, due to this development, contact with the spiritual world has gradually faded. Certainly, the gods were real to him, in so far as atheism was hardly conceivable in the Greek age, but gods were no longer felt to be real in the same sense. They became shadow-like. Hence the famous Greek expression, "It is better to be a beggar on earth than a king in the kingdom of shadows."

Again we must imagine what illnesses were like during the Greek era. We have given a few suggestions, but they do not represent the real picture of illness as a whole. We must limit ourselves again to the expression, "deformation." As we still are not able to give a clear-cut description of the deformation, it is followed in the diagram by a question mark. Our diagram develops accordingly:

Treatment	Illness	Humanity
	Egypt	

Temple sleep -------- Deformations (?) --- Connected with the gods
Prayers
Herbs
  ?

| | **Greece** | |

Temple sleep (dreams) – Deformations (?) -- Acquainted with the gods
Prayers
Herbs
Laying on of hands
Baths
Diets
Way of Life

An Important Interval

Let us try to understand more clearly the expression "connected with the gods," which we used for the Egyptian era. How might people in ancient times have approached spiritual beings? We hear about three ways:

1) By seeing visions, constantly mentioned throughout the Old Testament;
2) By hearing voices, as when people hear the voice of God (e.g., Samuel heard his name called);
3) By immediate contact or touching (e.g., Jacob wrestling with the Angel).

Of course we must translate this information into our own terms. These means of communication partake of the world of the senses, which was the only way to make them understandable to man living in that world. The change of consciousness in the Greek age is expressed by using the phrase "acquainted with the Gods" instead of, as in the Egyptian era, "connected with the gods." What does this mean? People increasingly lost their connection with the spiritual world. It is not the place here to elaborate on the organic, the bodily side of this problem; some reference to this has been made in the first chapter. The conscious connection with the spiritual world is possible only through organs which, in all times of the past and still throughout the Orient at present, are known as Lotus-flowers. We must imagine, therefore, that these organs gradually withered away or "deteriorated."

Now we are able to express in words what has happened: humanity has gone from a state of being "heaven-connected" to being "earth-directed." He has turned himself toward the earth. This has already been indicated in the introductory section in which we spoke about the transition from ancient times to the period introduced by Aristotle. If we stand straight and direct our gaze toward the sky, and if we then bend our heads downward, we experience in physical movement what happened at that time spiritually: the direct connection with spiritual beings was severed, and thus the ability to receive impressions, hear voices, and, finally, experience visions was lost.

In earlier times, when man was in contact with spiritual beings, he was safeguarded against going astray in the world of desires, which is spoken of as the world of sin. This is the reason that the old kings, the leaders, were judges at the same time. We have a wonderful example of the old leadership when we think of Moses, who had to master or, we could say, had to keep an eye on, the behavior of his people. They could not yet be responsible for their own actions. The moment Moses turned his back to ascend Mount Sinai to receive the Ten Commandments (again we need not take these matters literally, but at least we can attend to the events), a disaster took place down below: the worship of the golden calf, a picture of the loss of control.

To summarize these few points, man started to bend down toward the earth, he lost spiritual hearing, he lost spiritual vision. His passions and desires threatened to take possession of him. The consequence that threatened was that man would not be able to continue his evolution; his very development was threatened.

To summarize in different words: people became bent, crooked; they became deaf; they became blind; they became possessed; and, finally, they became paralyzed. These five characterizations are used purposely. Those familiar with the New Testament may even be surprised when they recognize the five examples of illnesses mentioned in connection with the healings of Christ. We encounter a great problem in our days. People who occupy themselves with the New Testament, who take the contents of the Bible seriously, ask me how I can understand the words crooked, deaf, blind, possessed, and paralyzed in the way I do. Must we not think, when hearing the word crooked, of an illness of the spine; when we hear about deafness, of an illness like otosclerosis; when we hear about blindness, of an illness like a cataract; when we hear about being possessed, of an illness such as schizophrenia; when we hear about being paralyzed, of a destructive illness of the central nervous system?

Let us imagine for a moment that the illnesses in question really are of a physical nature! Here we meet two attitudes. Those who stand firmly on the basis of modern materialistic thinking and consider themselves healthy realists will say, "To the best of my knowledge, I cannot imagine that such a physical deformation could ever be healed all of a sudden, as is described in the New Testament." Those who are convinced of the truth of everything that is described in the New Testament will say, "This is exactly what we regard as miracles. Such is the force of our belief that we are able to accept these miracles in spite of the contradiction with our modern knowledge." I am of the opinion that these two viewpoints will never meet. They have one thing in common, however: both begin from the same premise, that the illnesses mentioned in the healings of Christ can, should, or must be considered as illnesses *as we know them nowadays.*

In trying to find a solution to this problem, I experienced something very special. At first, I myself had the greatest difficulty in imagining that Christ would have been able to perform something that I could only call sorcery. I was forced to think along these lines as long as I imagined that intense physical deformations had been taken away suddenly in these healings. My own knowledge of laws in the world of everyday life, which I met as a physician, erected a firm obstacle to such a view. When I describe the illnesses as spiritual, in the way I have just done, this could be considered as seeking a compromise. Such a reproach is understandable, but as an enemy of compromises I must tell you why I claim the right to look at things in the way I have. This leads to a very special example among the illnesses that were healed by Christ, one that has not been mentioned yet, an illness of which both parties described just now would say, "There you are; here we have an illness that we definitely can say is a real, visible, concrete, terrible deformation." I am referring to leprosy. Christ healed the people suffering from this disease. For me, also, there was no way out of this difficulty.

The answer to this problem came to me about ten years ago when I had a surprising discussion with a Jewish friend of mine, who is considered one of the most learned scientific linguists, especially in classics and old Hebrew languages. Without any connection to the question of illness, he said to me, "If you Christians only knew how badly your New Testament has been translated. Your word "leprosy," for instance, has no relation whatsoever to the original word *tsoraäth*." He continued, "*Tsoraäth* means something that begins to become visible; you could consider *tsoraäth* in this case to be an illness that just begins to show itself on the outside of the body." In this sense, all modern illnesses with clear visible symptoms are *tsoraäth*.

I hope it is evident how much this answer was a solution to my problem. I found justification for a thought that I can now declare openly: in those days man in general did not yet have the illnesses we have now. We must understand that this was the time, the turning point, in which illnesses began to become more visible, more concrete, more physical, and eventually more destructive than before. We will see that this supposition will be justified still more in the course of our further investigations.

Two illustrations from the New Testament will reinforce the suggestion that we should try to look on the healings of Christ in another, less physical way. First of all, Christ revived the little daughter of Jaïrus, who was twelve years old. Immediately after this event comes the healing of the woman who had suffered from bleeding for twelve years. Here we find a touching image and an example of the interplay of forces: in the first case, the child was not able to reach puberty, or a ripeness in earthly life and a connection with earthly laws; in the other case, earthly influences had too strong a hold on a human being, and she could not free herself.

A further contrast is given by two other patients, a man who is too "watery" (Luke 14:1-6) and a woman who is too "dry" (Luke 13:10-17). I think it is not difficult to understand that each shows the opposite of what we expect in healthy life: a woman is generally more cosmic, softer (more "watery"), and a man is generally more earthly, more solid (more "dry").

In both examples we find the same thing: the creation of a balance between cosmic and earthly forces in man, in preparation for a future epoch. Humanity was preparing itself to become fit for a life on earth separated from the cosmos and therefore able to develop freedom and independence.

The source of healing characterizes the difference between healing in the preceding Greek and Egyptian periods and in the era of Christ. In what way was Christ able to heal deformations? When we described temple sleep and temple dream we spoke about healing through divine forces. We find a satisfying answer to the question when we presume that the ancient healing forces, which worked as cosmic forces in man during his sleep, were closely related, even similar perhaps, to the forces that radiated from Christ. In healing through temple sleep we could even speak of a "healing heaven." Christ's healing could be seen as heaven coming toward the earth!

We can, however, be more exact in looking at healing as it developed from ancient to Christian times. In earlier times, healing was performed in a passive manner; the sick in the temples were simply healed. Christ also healed the sick, but here, for the first time, a new element entered. We have seen that humanity had, for the most part, lost its conscious connection with the spiritual world. At the same time, we can understand that only those in whom a remnant of the old consciousness still lived could be healed. This may be expressed in the words,

"Your faith has healed you." This means we must learn to understand that Christ could not heal everybody. Christ asks, "Will you be healed?" and after the healing comes the condition, "Sin no more." What we see is that a new element in humanity is being called upon, an element that was not present before in evolution. "Sin no more" implies that before that time man was not yet able *not* to sin. The people are no longer merely guided by the shepherd-kings. Humanity has gained the capacity not to sin. This new, divine principle had started to seek out a dwelling place in man. We actually can speak of a new birth. It is out of this principle, as articulated by Paul at a very particular moment in the words, "Not I, but Christ in me," that humanity became responsible for its actions.

I feel it necessary to clarify this a bit further, because it might look as if I did not consider the illnesses that were healed by Christ as physical illnesses, though I spoke of them as deformations. Here I must make a correction. When I compare "to be crooked," "to be deaf," "to be blind," "to be possessed," and "to be paralyzed" with psychic conditions that have gradually appeared in the course of time, I also presume that some form of physical condensation of these conditions was experienced as well. In this connection, it is interesting to remind ourselves of the descriptions of healing through temple dream during the Greek time as in Epidaurus, for example, and to discover that the illnesses described there are mostly the same illnesses (not always) that we meet in the Bible. This indicates to me that the assumption that these illnesses parallel the change in man's consciousness gains more ground.

In any event, we read about illnesses that are described as blindness, deafness, paralysis, etc. What do these words mean? First of all, they express a condition; we have no idea at all what sort of illness, in the sense of our modern diagnosis, caused that blindness, deafness, etc. If Christ took earth mixed with saliva and put it on the eyes, this certainly suggests a physical treatment. Yet are we really satisfied in thinking that applying earth mixed with saliva can heal a physical illness? Many a religious person could ask if Christ was truly in need of these physical substances. Wasn't He capable of healing without this medium, even if these illnesses were just as concrete as we know them to be nowadays? If, on the other hand, we take these illnesses as hidden "deformations," as we have called them in the Egyptian and early Greek eras, why did Christ make use of this physical treatment at all?

I would never think, of course, of trying to give any definite answer. My own conclusion is that we will have to accept the fact that a change in man's consciousness is accompanied by a change in his physical condition. The physical deformations that were found in reality, how ever, *can never be traced again.* When I think of the ex pressions, possessed, blind, deaf, etc., and also the con cept of the *tsoraäth,* as I have described it, I feel that this sets the limits to my investigation. The fact that nowa days—2,000 years later—we are confronted with a total ly different situation, confronted with many more destructive illnesses of which we have gathered such an exact knowledge, may enable us to understand how much man's constitution has changed. The illnesses of our time did not yet exist in those days. We have to do with a marvelous picture in which every detail must be seen in its proper place, in connection with the others, so that we experience a reality, not by reading the descriptions as such but by feeling that the truth is revealed *between* the facts. We will be able later to elaborate on this principle in a still more extensive way.

When we return to our studies of medicine, from which we deviated in exploring the events in Palestine, we must never forget that, in spite of the influence these happenings have had in the world regarding the foundation of Christianity, in the course of history they have not had the slightest influence on the development of medicine. The impulse that was given by Christ had to await its time to be recognized. In adding this "hidden impulse" to our diagram, I have written the word Palestine.

Treatment	Illness	Humanity
	Egypt	
Temple sleep ————————	Deformations (?) ———	Connected with the gods
Prayers		
Herbs		
?		
	Greece	
Temple sleep (dreams)–	Deformations (?) ———	Acquainted with the gods
Prayers		
Herbs		
Laying on of hands		
Baths		
Diets		
Way of Life		
	Palestine	

Europe: Medicine after Hippocrates

The development of modern medicine went its own way, but we cannot go into too many details. I would like simply to distinguish a few more-or-less clear episodes in the development of medicine during the more than twenty centuries since Hippocrates. Hippocrates himself represents, as we have seen, the beginning of modern medicine in Greek times. The center of medical knowledge gradually shifted to Alexandria, and we begin to speak of the Hellenistic time. This was followed by a Roman period, which gradually merged with medical developments in Europe. The progress in Europe was strongly influenced for many centuries by Arabic science. After the Arabic influence we discover that medical science developed more and more concepts and experiences, which eventually led to the great change in consciousness seen most clearly in the rise of a materialistic attitude.

When we occupy ourselves with the conception of illness itself, we remember that Hippocrates considered health and illness to be the result of a good or a bad mixture of black gall, yellow gall, phlegm, and blood. We find the same conception in Galenus, who was born about a hundred years after Christ. Believe it or not, nearly 1,000 years later, Avicenna—the great Arabian physician—spoke of illness in exactly the same way. This knowledge is even carried on for the four following centuries. Is it not remarkable that the same conception kept the world of medicine in fetters for nearly 2,000 years? Can we develop some understanding of this fact?

What about the medicines that were used over this long, long period? Already in the Hellenistic times we find an intensive trade in herbs and natural substances used in medicine. Alexandria was a great center, situated in the midst of Asia, Africa, and Europe. Where did these plants and herbs come from, how were they discovered, how did man know about their effects? Certainly not by our means of investigation, and certainly not by chance. We should never project our modern views and attitude toward our environment into the past. Actually, we came across the discovery of herbs at the time of the Egyptian temple healing. To call this an instinctive mode of discovery is perhaps the best way to speak of it.

It is not difficult to imagine that a certain instinctive consciousness existed in those days in many persons who had a close connection with the natural environment. When we accept the idea that also in the later centuries the capacity remained alive to find plants used for healing purposes in a more-or-less intuitive way, we are reminded of the fact that we still have persons in our midst who have a special feeling for plants that we can definitely distinguish from what we call exact knowledge. Some years ago, a booklet on herbs by Mellie Uijldert appeared in Holland, called *The Language of the Herbs*. Clearly, she was not a scientist. A modern scientist would never allow himself to speak about a "language of plants." He would be interested in biochemical compounds only.

To elucidate further the change that took place in humanity in the course of time, we could say that man's increasing knowledge in thinking and differentiation took the place of his original awareness of supersensible realities. From head to foot he became a sober, earthly being. The last remnants of earlier consciousness were kept only in the tips of his fingers. "Herbalists," who we still find here and there, are often said to have "a green thumb" or in German, *"Fingerspitzengefühl,"* "feeling fingertips."

What does this short investigation show? We must confess that the many herbs that have been used in medicine for thousands of years and that, as we saw in the beginning, have nearly disappeared in our time, were found by methods that man cannot apply any longer to the kingdoms of nature. This is the reason that man gradually stopped making use of herbs. He had lost a feeling for nature, and he had lost confidence. He could no longer work with them, because his consciousness had changed. This is why one rarely hears of great medical discoveries in the periods after the Greeks.

Could it be that the persistence of the idea that illnesses were caused by a wrong mixture of black gall, yellow gall, phlegm, and blood accorded with tradition in the field of medicine? If herbs were added to the stock of medicines, it was not done by those who were the real representatives of the official medical science but by those people one would now call herbalists, who still had more-or-less atavistic capacities.

As we have mentioned, other medical treatments were used in the Greek era, such as laying on of hands, baths, diets, "way of life" prescriptions, but we should note that entirely new medical treatments, as we would consider them to be now, did not appear. When, for instance, the metal mercury appeared at a certain moment in the treatment of syphilis, the real origin of its use lies in the dark. Maybe we should look toward the alchemists, who may have discovered other mineral substances that were used for healing, but again we must emphasize that alchemists were not recognized physicians. They led their own lives and were, in spite of later degeneration, devoted to the divine forces in nature.

Just as we have seen that in the conception of illness we find a strong tradition that lasted for centuries, we may say that also in the field of treatments tradition played an important part. Tradition, however, means something built on the past and having no strength of renewal in itself. Of course, as we will see later, there have been exceptions, persons who rejected tradition, who tried new ideas, but on the whole we cannot deny that tradition was the leading power.

What about humanity's attitude toward the spiritual world, toward the divine? We find a clear transition: in Egypt, fully connected with the gods, in Greece, acquainted with the gods; now we meet a third form in which I, for the first time, would like to use the word "religion": "believing in God," or religion, as we call it. The beginning of all these religions lies in the past, as we have described in the section, "Knowing and Believing." Here we may also introduce the word "dogma." Are not all religions in the world, including the Christian denominations, permeated with dogma? The beginning of Christianity lies in the Greek era. We can feel how closely tradition and dogma are connected.

We have laid out a diagram with three headings; treatment, illness, and humanity. We still must question ourselves about illness. We concluded that we do not know what sort of illnesses were present during the Greek civilization and that we should limit ourselves to the word "deformation," but what illnesses do we know of in the times after the Greek civilization? In a short digression, we touched upon the healings of Christ, which allowed us to affirm the rightness of the word deformation, referring to something not really visible, as we would use the word nowadays.

Previously we made some remarks on the problem of discerning the character of illnesses in ancient times. We have already mentioned observations made about mummies and dead bodies, even fossilized ones, found in graves. It has been said that most of the physical ailments we hear of in ancient times are wounds or at least the result of wounds, which is quite reasonable, although in a certain way wounds are not really illnesses in the sense we have been using. Scientists inform us that an illness such as osteomyelitis (inflammation of the bone marrow), for instance, has been found in many cases.* Osteomyelitis, however, can be considered as a consequence of physical violence, e.g., wounds, which of course were quite common. Infections may certainly have been frequent.

Another illness of which we hear from the so-called Ebers Papyrus was described as a pathological abundance of urine. Even a special treatment was indicated: herbs in very special application and quantity were to be used, as well as invoking the gods with religious formulae. The Ebers Papyrus is officially regarded as proof that diabetes already existed. When speaking about diabetes and taking it for granted that we would have found the same anatomic changes in those days that we find today, I begin to have some misgivings. It could well be, however, that the same illness may have shown itself in subtle symptoms in the time of Egypt and showed many more concrete physical symptoms and more destructive effects later on.

Trepanations or artificial holes in skulls are often found. Investigators have even discovered little changes at the edges of the holes, which show that these holes must have been made during the lifetime. Their conclusion is that brain operations must have been performed. If,however, we imagine the amount of knowledge that is necessary for brain surgery, I think this goes too far. We simply do not know why these trepanations were made. Maybe they were skull injuries. Answering the question about which illnesses existed in those days will be possible only after we have studied the change in humanity in the course of history in many more respects.

We may for a moment call to mind what has been said about healing through temple sleep. Let us never

---

*Paul Hühnerfeld,

forget that healing in one night, practiced through thousands of years, presents us with a problem that cannot be solved with arguments taken from modern experiences. In every field man is passing through an evolution that leads him from cosmic realms into earthly conditions. As an example we should compare the physical body of a young child with that of an old man. We then can come to the conclusion that humanity has become more physical, hardened, "older." Later we will see that the increase in the frequency of very special illnesses today further supports this.

This change has not always taken place in the same way. From a group life, as we saw in the beginning, humanity gradually became more individualized. Certainly, at the time of Christ, there were already ailments of a more physical kind, although not quite as physical as we experience them nowadays. Those people had alienated themselves from the divine world at too early a stage. They "believed no more" and therefore could not be healed by Christ. Their inner attitude had built up a barrier that showed itself in a too-physical deformation.

Which illnesses do we hear of in the first millenium and even later? The answer can be short: mainly epidemics. It is instructive to know that even an illness such as syphilis originally appeared as an epidemic. The early epidemics consisted of the plague, smallpox, cholera, typhoid fever, and leprosy (the leprosy we know of today). Epidemics infested Europe, devastating at one time one fifth of Europe's entire population. There were other illnesses, of course, but if someone were to declare that many modern illnesses were already present, I would answer, certainly not with the same frequency. Modern, more exact illnesses appeared by and by. In a book by Beversluis (seventeenth century), the problem of tumors fills a very small space. In a volume by Rhazes, a great Arabian doctor, we find elaborate descriptions of smallpox and measles. Such writings present an accurate picture of the prevalence of inflammatory illnesses.

What caused these epidemics? They were regarded as a "scourge of God." The idea is not farfetched. On the contrary, the experience of fate-connected influences that man had to accept as part of his life was as old as humanity's history. Even at the beginning of the nineteenth century we encounter a remnant of this attitude, though instead of the "scourge of God" the physician used the expression "*genus epidemicus.*" The words were different, but they meant the same thing.

In the Egyptian and Greek times we spoke about deformations, without stating exactly what these deformations were. The causes came from within, from the inward life of the soul, which we have related to the fall of man into matter, to a concept of sin in the widest sense of the word. If an illness was caused by insobriety in any form, we had to do with a real problem of the character, of the soul itself. Of course, there were influences from the environment, which we have mentioned in the instance of malaria, but this was just an incipient problem. When the great epidemics began, however, we encounter a strong influence from without connecting with inner conditions. We will go more deeply into this subject later. The influences from without we would now call bacteria and the like, but in those days people had no notion of this. They were well aware of the contagious element that reigned in the big epidemics. They did not doubt for a moment, however, that these catastrophes were the consequence of man's sinful life. Hence, the expression: "scourge of God."

We thus begin to recognize clearly two factors in this

form of illness: one from within, which we have called deformation in speaking of the Egyptian and the Greek eras, and the other from without, showing itself in the contagious aspect of the epidemics. This consideration will prove to be fruitful when we come to speak of modern conceptions of illness as derived from external as well as internal causes.

We can now extend our original diagram in the following way:

Treatment   **Illness**   **Humanity**

Egypt

Temple sleep ———————   Deformations (?) ———Connected with the gods
Prayers
Herbs
  ?

Greece

Temple sleep (dreams)– Deformations (?) ——Acquainted with the gods
Prayers
Herbs
Laying on of hands
Baths
Diets
Way of Life

Palestine

Europe
(until nineteenth century)

Tradition ——————————   Epidemics   ———————— Believing in God
                                        (Scourge of God)   (Dogma)
                                        (*Genus Epidemicus*)

The question arises, what were the main achievements in medical science during these times? These achievements lie in the field of anatomy and physiology. Everyone knows about the incredible increase of knowledge in these fields. In medical history we find many examples of such achievements already in the early days. We have mentioned the Hellenistic era and may now mention two names, Herophilos and Erasistratos, both living in the third century. Herophilos, the first to dissect corpses, wrote an extensive book on anatomy; he distinguished for the first time between sensory and motor nerves and thoroughly examined the pulse qualities in different illnesses. Erasistratos was the first to describe the connections between the convolutions of the brain and intelligence.

In the Roman times, Epicurus (physicians in those days were often philosophers as well) was among the first to apply psychic treatments. The background of his treatment was based on three principles: there is only one source of knowledge and that is sense perception; there is only one anxiety in life, fear of the gods and fear of death; there is only one aim worthwhile in life, striving for well-being. I think we can easily see how much human consciousness already differs from ancient times. This Epicurus, living three centuries before Christ, taught that fear of the gods was senseless, because the gods did not care about us. The fear of death was senseless, for as long as we live, death is absent; when death is finally present, we won't "be" anymore. In short, illness is listlessness, health is well-being.

In the first century after Christ we meet the great Galenus of Pergamon, one of the most brilliant personalities in the history of medicine and a person whose authority lasted for centuries. As we have seen, however, he too still based his medical practice on the doctrine of the four liquids of Hippocrates. The wrong mixture of these liquids he called *dyskrasia*, which meant illness. The treatment of the patient consisted of the establishment of the right mixture, which generally meant a reintegration of man with nature. He described the human constitution in connection with the temperaments: in the melancholic, the black gall was predominant; in the sanguine, the blood; in the phlegmatic, the phlegm; and finally he spoke of the choleric, suffering from too much yellow gall.

What I would like to point out is that, at the time of Galenus, we find a continuation of some kind of conception of man and nature that carries on with unbelievable force until the fourteenth century; it is still living even in the soul of a personality like Paracelsus, of whom we will speak in the following section. As we have seen, however, the origin of it all lies in the time of Hippocrates. "*Hippos*," the horse image of the old cosmic wisdom, still influenced man as he entered a new era— the era of exact knowledge—and forgot (probably because he had to) about the spiritual world in order to get to know and develop exactness and discrimination in the world of the senses. This becomes his reality.

Galenus developed a deeper insight into physiology, digestion, the function of the liver in the blood production, the relationship between respiration and blood circulation, and so on. He thought about, explored, discovered, and brought to awareness many problems in the field of knowledge with which one is familiar nowadays. As Hühnerfeld wrote, "The physiology of Galenus was a work of genius. His main importance lies in the fact that he felt that medicine needed to rest on a firm basis of human physiology and that physicians should understand the relationships among nutrition, respiration, and circulation."* We may explicitly mention his daring suppositions in the realm of anatomy, although he never dissected a dead body! We must appreciate the statements and knowledge of such a man against the background of his time.

Around the tenth century, Arabic science appears. The two outstanding figures of this period were Rhazes and Avicenna. Rhazes wrote a medical encyclopedia; Avicenna put together a compendium of the achievements of anatomical and physiological investigations. As far as the conception of illness was concerned, however, the causes were still believed to originate in an incorrect mixture of black gall, yellow gall, phlegm, and blood.

The great jump in the field of knowledge concerning the human body began during the time of Leonardo da Vinci and Vesalius. Leonardo's explorations in human anatomy and physiology are world renowned. Vesalius' *Textbook of Anatomy* is a masterpiece. These individuals are followed by personalities such as Galileo, Newton, and Harvey, the great British physician. Harvey was the first to discover the connection between the blood circulation and the heart beat. (Galenus considered the stream of the blood as the rise and fall of rhythmic vital impulses.) He also wrote a book on the origin of man.

In the middle of the seventeenth century, Sydenham became world-famous for his extensive description of gout, also mentioning the connection between gout and one's "way of life."

Von Haller (1708-1777) made a thorough study of the functions of the lungs and the muscles. Van Swieten (1700-1777), who practiced in Vienna, was the first

_____
*Paul Hühnerfeld,

organizer of modern clinical medicine. His way of making records of patients, their biographies, their symptoms, diagnoses and prognoses, indications for treatments, etc. was outstanding. Both von Haller and van Swieten were pupils of the famous Dutch physician, Boerhaave (1668-1738), in Leyden. He was in his time a personality of great repute. Every important person who sought help visited, if at all possible, Boerhaave. He was above all a doctor, a man of strong will and character. It is interesting that we so often hear the expression "celebrated doctors." In spite of the fact that we often hear about their fame and great medical successes, however, we never hear details about what they did, or which medicine they prescribed. Why not? Because—let us stress it again—what they prescribed was based on tradition. That was not the special reason for their success. Just as the teachings of Hippocrates influenced medicine for about 2,000 years, so the knowledge of herbs and other treatments was passed down through the centuries, because no *new* knowledge of medicine had developed. A new knowledge, a new approach to medical science, had to await its time.

We speak of healing, however, and therefore we may assume that these great doctors still bore a quality in their souls. Something of the past, of the time when healing still drew on higher forces, streamed from their whole being. Even today we meet doctors who, by nature, create that wonderful atmosphere of rest and confidence that works as a blessing and cure for those around them. Everyone will have met or heard about some doctor of whom it is said, "When he enters the room, you are already half-healed."

I only mention this to show that famous doctors like Boerhaave, though not possessing a sophisticated selection of effective medicines, still had an inkling of what healing was. A well-known Dutch physician, J.H. van den Berg, once stated in his book, *Medical Power and Medical Ethics* (which I recommend to everyone), "We now know how to heal, but we are not good doctors. In ancient times there were good doctors, but of course they did not know how to heal." It is clear that I cannot agree with this statement; on the contrary, I would like to emphasize that those "good doctors in ancient times" still had the capacity for healing as a last ray of light from the past. To what extent, on the other hand, the great achievements in modern medicine can really be called "healing" is another problem. The question asked in the beginning of this book—"Are we on the right path?"—should be kept in mind continually.

Paracelsus, van Helmont, Hahnemann

Before going on to the compelling events of which we will soon speak, we must take a final look back. We should not forget that not everyone fitted into the scheme of tradition. There were always personalities who felt the decline of their time and who strongly objected to the course of events. Three individuals may be mentioned; there certainly have been more. The first is Paracelsus. He lived from the end of the fifteenth century into the sixteenth. IIis personality can best be characterized in one sentence: he strove with all his might against tradition. Imagine how a physician of his time looked. He was a dignified gentleman, either walking or being driven, dressed in a long coat, wearing a special doctor's hat, speaking measured and respectable latin. (At universities all medical teaching was in Latin.) Paracelsus was a rebel. Of Swiss origin, square-built with a big nose, fiery eyes, and thick lips, he seemed more a peasant than the civilized doctor one expected. During his medical studies he developed an extraordinary knowledge of plants and herbs. He studied people thoroughly, not referring to traditional conceptions. His main concern was to "conquer" tradition; to study plants, animals, and man anew, "to pass the examination of nature," as he called it.

He spoke of five divine principles that work in nature and in man; he called them *"entia"* and referred to them in the following way:

Ens astrale: the human being is the result of the influence of the stars, in other words, of the creating beings;

Ens naturale: in the realm of human biography, each man is a world in himself, a microcosm;

Ens veneni: Paracelsus referred here, in all probability, to the realm of the metabolic processes in man, nutrition included;

Ens spirituale: man is a spiritual being able to perceive and think about the world.

Ens dei: this is the element in the human being from which the force of healing issues.

Paracelsus claimed anew that the origin of healing is in the divine. He spoke of the "Archaeus," meaning the element of life, as a reality of its own. Salt (sal), mercury, and sulphur are the three principles of which every substance, every being on earth, consists—salt, the principle between earth and water; mercury, the principle between water and air; sulphur, the principle between air and warmth.

Earth, water, air, and warmth are the last substances, the ultimate matter. Salt, mercury, sulphur, the first substances, are the primary matter. They are not chemical substances; they are processes of transition between the physical appearances: the four elements of earth, water, air, and warmth.

If we write down the four ultimate "matter"-substances,

```
warmth
air
water
earth
```

and we add to this diagram the primary "matter"-substances, we could write:

```
warmth
         _____    sulphur
air
         _____    mercury
water
         _____    salt
earth
```

We have a picture of the four earthly realities with gaps in between. In the gaps that separate them, we find the processes of sulphur, mercury, and salt. Paracelsus even gave an example of these processes becoming visible, as shown in the following diagram:

```
warmth
         _____    sulphur    _____    flower  ⎞
air                                                   ⎟ of the
         _____    mercury    _____    leaves  ⎬
water                                                 ⎟ plant
         _____    salt       _____    root    ⎠
earth
```

We will return to this example later (in the section on illness), extending it into the realm of the human body.

Paracelsus spoke German in his lectures and fumed about the methods, behavior, and treatments of his colleagues. He was not much beloved, and he was as much rejected as admired by his contemporaries. Finally, it is said that he was murdered, leaving behind him many, many books that are still studied today. His personality must have worked in a surprising way; he who reads his books will have difficulty fully understanding what Paracelsus meant. We feel that Paracelsus struggled for the right words to express what can never be expressed in clear-cut language. Rather, his meaning comes to us as a revelation, just as we experience a work of art. In the work of Paracelsus we feel that something is revealing itself that can never be said in exact words. It is good to realize that words can never express truth itself. Words can only circumscribe; the reality of a thought, of an idea, of truth, is revealed *between* words, in the same way as the essence of a symphony lies between the tones.

We feel that Paracelsus tried to recollect or reinforce something in himself that elsewhere was dying out. The question arises, however: was he trying to hold on to something doomed to disappear or was he anticipating something to be developed in the future?

A second remarkable personality is John Baptist van Helmont, who lived at the end of the sixteenth century and into the seventeenth (approximately one century after Paracelsus). His interest in medicine was stimulated by his knowledge of plants. In many ways he was deeply disturbed by the state of medicine that he experienced in his days. He was very unhappy indeed about the discrepancy between discussing medicine in an eloquent and sophisticated manner and yet being unable to cure even a toothache or scabies. Let us not forget the well-known expression of those days, "to lie like a doctor." People felt the emptiness that was hidden in the coat, hat, behavior, and incomprehensible language of physicians; they felt the hypocrisy.

It is stated that van Helmont was inspired by a dream in which he was told that he would possess the power of the Archangel Raphael and the divine medicine if he were to become a doctor. It is not surprising that he did not base his knowledge and conviction on the well-known doctors of his time but on Paracelsus and Hippocrates. He also spoke of Archaeus and the element of life as a reality in man. He considered illness to be a disturbance of the life processes, but life processes could be disturbed only by something of the same nature. We might presume that van Helmont tried to understand that something must work directly in the field of life and must therefore have certain qualities. He took a great interest in chemistry; following in the footsteps of Paracelsus, however, he never tried to explain life in terms of chemical processes, and he strongly objected to those who considered the human body a mere mechanism. Following the same line of investigation, we see again in van Helmont someone who strove to keep contact with the non-physical, divine element in man.

The third individuality is Samuel Hahnemann, the founder of homeopathy. Hahnemann's main concern was "life." Life he saw as something outside the rational, something that was a reality in itself. He worked in the realm of diluted medicines, the so-called homeopathic solutions, which were based on experiments. By taking small quantities of some herb or chemical substance over a certain period of time, he experienced in himself bodily sensations that he compared with symptoms of well-known illnesses. Eventually, he succeeded in healing these illnesses by giving the related substances in high dilutions (potencies). The similarity he discovered between the symptoms of an illness and those caused by a particular medicament led to his conclusion that "the same is healed by the same" (*similia similibus curentur*). In Hahnemann's use of dilutions, we see someone who seems to be trying to build a bridge between the physical and the non-physical worlds. I have the impression that for Hahnemann the physical world was in a way a condensation of divine activities from a supersensible reality. In making his dilutions, it was as though he had the intuitive feeling that he was delivering the essence of a substance out of its solid state.

Hahnemann (1755-1843), living about two hundred

years later than van Helmont, was a totally different individual from his two predecessors. He was a brilliant
personality of great fame, and he began a new trend in
medicine as the inventor of homeopathic treatment. He
was strict about his principles, especially as far as
homeopathy was concerned. If one of his pupils dared use
a non-homeopathic medicine, he could be certain of his
master's wrath. In some places in Germany, there were
clearly two parties, one for and one against Hahnemann.
In many ways, though, he ploughed a lonely furrow. At
eighty years of age, he suddenly vanished overnight and
reappeared in Paris, where he began a new practice with
great display. For eight years, he and his young wife pre-
sided over most of the medical life there. He then died,
and his young wife sank into oblivion.

We will see later how much we may regard these
three individuals (of course there are many more) as not
only opposing the opinions of their time but also anticipating new impulses to come.

The Nineteenth Century

Where does this lead us? What happened to the traditional application of early medicines? We have already
seen that uncertainty about the question, "Can we heal at
all?" was widespread due to the nihilism of the nineteenth century, when physicians lost their confidence in
traditional methods that had prevailed for 2,000 years.
These traditions originated in times into which science
does not penetrate, because it bases itself on exact knowledge of the physical world alone.

What is the cause of illness? We have spoken about
the "*genus epidemicus*," and now we must look at the
fact that in the midst of the last century the existence of
bacteria was discovered. In the beginning not everyone
could accept that the final cause of many illnesses lay

here. In modern times we are so accustomed to this thought, we are so used to the idea that the flu is caused by a virus, that it is difficult for us to imagine that people did not feel, when they heard of this discovery, that at last they had found what they had been looking for!

On the contrary, it took several years for many doctors to overcome their difficulty in accepting a conception that was the reverse of an earlier conviction; there was a strong resistance to discarding all at once the belief in a divine origin of illness. We may express this attitude in our diagram in the same way we express the doubt about the ability to heal, by putting a question mark in both cases (see page 79).

There is a third question mark, however, to be added to our diagram. As long as man was related to the divine world, in some way or other, if only in the form of a traditional religion or in the form of a dogma, man was still confident that he came from a spiritual world, that he was a creation of God. Even Darwin had this view. The second edition of his book, *The Origin of Species*, bore the title *The Origin of Species out of God*. The word "God" still had a real meaning for him.

To illustrate what happened at the end of the last century, I would like to tell a little story that is part of a book by a famous Dutch author, Multatuli (1820-1887). He wrote *"Woutertje Pieterse"* (The Story of Little Walter). It goes as follows:

Mrs. Pieterse has invited a number of lay-friends to show off her eldest son, Stoffel, who has just become a schoolmaster, trained by the old schoolmaster of the village, Mr. Pennewip. The ladies sit in the room, talking, chatting, and drinking hot milk with slempsyrup—an old-fashioned sweet syrup—while Mrs. Pieterse begins to brag about her big son, who is sitting in a corner smoking his long Gouda-pipe. "He is so clever," she says, "He knows that nouns are male or female. Even verbs are male or female." She muses, "He is such a learned man. There is even more. You will be greatly surprised." She now addresses another lady, Miss Laps. "For instance, you, Miss Laps, you would be surprised to know what you are." "Well," says Miss Laps, "I suppose I am Miss Laps." "Oh no," says Mrs. Pieterse, "That is your name. I mean what you are in reality." "Well, I am a Catholic," answers Miss Laps. "Oh no, my dear, I mean something totally different; please Stoffel, do tell her what she is." Stoffel takes his pipe out of his mouth and says in a slow, clear voice, "Miss Laps, you are a mammal."

The effect is shocking. Miss Laps jumps to her feet and shouts furiously, "This is a terrible lie. I have always been a decent woman. My father was a wheat trader. You should be ashamed of yourself." Her face is red, she trembles all over, continuing her voluble speech. All the ladies join the discussion. There is a terrible hullabaloo. Everyone shouts while Mrs. Pieterse tries in vain to calm the chaos. She is desperate, the whole evening is spoiled, and she had meant so well. Only Stoffel sits quietly aside, hiding himself in a cloud of smoke.

At that moment there is a knock at the door. All of a sudden the room falls silent. The door is opened and Mr. Pennewip enters, the old bearded schoolmaster. The reason he comes need not bother us, but Mrs. Pieterse immediately sees her chance and addresses him quickly, "Isn't it true, Mr. Pennewip, that Miss Laps is a mammal?" Mr. Pennewip slowly and solemnly walks up to Miss Laps, who still sits trembling and red-faced in her chair. He bends down to her, introduces himself, asks her name, and continues, "Miss Laps, do you breathe through gills?" She did not. "Miss Laps, do you live sometimes in the water and sometimes on land?" She did not. "Well, Miss Laps, this will be my third and decisive question: Can you lay eggs?" She could not. "Then, Miss Laps, you are a mammal." Miss Laps had no answer for that.

I do not quote this story to surprise the reader with the fact that he is called a mammal. Nearly everyone nowadays knows that. What is important is that we should be aware of what it meant to people to experience the transition from being called a divine being to being considered merely the result of the evolution of animals. Remember for a moment that in the beginning of this book we mentioned the fact that it is not scientific any longer to speak about a Creator; we mentioned the expression "no watchmaker." Man became merely the chance result of a natural, physical process. The average man could not believe this in the beginning. "Am I not a divine being? Am I just some sort of an animal?" Here we touch upon the third question mark, as we complete our diagram of the nineteenth century.

Treatment	Illness	Humanity

Egypt

Temple sleep -------- Deformations (?) ---Connected with the gods
Prayers
Herbs
 ?

Greece

Temple sleep (dreams) - Deformations (?) --Acquainted with the gods
Prayers
Herbs
Laying on of hands
Baths
Diets
Way of Life

Palestine

Europe
(until nineteenth century)

Tradition ----------   Epidemics   ---------- Believing in God
                  (Scourge of God)   (Dogma)
                  (*Genus Epidemicus*)

Nineteenth Century

Can we heal? -- Are illnesses caused by bacteria? --Is man an animal?
(Doubting God)

What did this development mean? It was as if in the nineteenth century European culture held its breath. Old conceptions had lost their value.

The Dramatic Transition to the Twentieth Century

Let us remind ourselves of the three question marks in the diagram, indicating the situation in the nineteenth century, and let us also not forget the past, out of which these question marks gradually arose. We have been able to come to such a conclusion only because we began our investigations in the Egyptian era, whereas modern medicine considers the time of Hippocrates as its beginning point, not taking into account the time before Hippocrates. In surveying the total picture from Egypt up to our question marks and sensing the great transition in the time of Hippocrates, we may come to the conclusion that *modern medicine finds its beginning in the time of Hippocrates, the same time in which man gradually began to forget about healing.*

I can understand the attitude of nihilism only when I connect it with the change in ideas about illness and the change in the conception of the human being through the course of time: humanity gradually forgot about the existence of the spiritual world. I do not think, however, that we should conclude that this development should not have occurred. If modern man feels himself superior to his ancestors, having evolved and developed the force of thinking, of differentiation, and having created the world of exact science, I can indeed appreciate this view. We cannot forget nor deny, however, the almost dramatic conclusion that, in the nineteenth century, man went so far as to give up hope of ever being able to cure; hence the observation that it was as if European culture held its breath.

We have seen how much this attitude changed in the beginning of this century. From 1920 onward, the medical world took a totally new approach to illnesses and discovered totally new possibilities for treatment. An extraordinary number of medicines appeared in a relatively short time. We have also seen that the former attitude of modesty has become one of pride. Should we wonder? Does it not make sense that the medical world gradually came to the conviction that it would only be a matter of time until it could find an adequate treatment for every illness?

In looking at the conception of illness and its causes, we see that it is no longer a question of the "scourge of God," no longer a question of "*genus epidemicus*," but a matter of clear-cut knowledge. The causes of illness are from without: chemical, physical, biological, psychological, hereditary influences.* We really may say that in this change the traditional values were finally and completely cast aside. On the whole, the great change that

---

*In this conception I must consider hereditary influences also to be working from without. See the section on the course of human life.

has taken place in our century means that the fetters that man could no longer bear have been thrown off. Diagnosis itself has also undergone an unexpected enlargement, especially in the development of pathological anatomy, microscopic research, biophysics, and biochemistry.

It is good to keep in mind how relatively quickly the increase in knowledge has taken place. Although we have seen that many scientists in the field of medicine after the twelfth century contributed greatly to the knowledge of anatomy and physiology, the major increase in knowledge came only in the second half of the nineteenth and in the beginning of the twentieth centuries. Here arose a danger, however. We might recall that in early times illness took place mainly inside the body; hence the word *tsoraäth*, indicating a gradual increase in external symptoms. These symptoms, however, were merely the visible, outward signs of inward processes, processes that have been described as deformations, which resulted from what has been referred to as moral qualities (the fall of man). *Tsoraäth* meant that something invisible became visible; something inward became outward. In our day, we have come to see illness as the sum of the symptoms themselves. (Courvoisier, Napoleon's doctor, promulgated this conception of illness.) Illness thus came to be regarded very simply as "bad luck," a nuisance that man had to overcome as soon as possible; that is, illness was not meant to be! Here we find the root of the so-called symptomatic treatments of our day.

Concerning the illnesses themselves, we are dealing with a subtle subject. When we mention the increase of cancer, for instance, many a scientist is inclined to answer that this apparent increase is simply a question of an improvement in diagnosing. I fear this is wishful thinking. Indeed, it would simplify the problem to suggest that humanity always encountered more or less the same illnesses. When we look at the increase in rheumatic illnesses, heart and vessel diseases, illnesses of the central nervous system, we gradually understand that an increase in cancer is not an isolated phenomenon but part of an important change in humanity's whole condition.

We come now to the change of attitude toward the origin of the human being. The little story of Miss Laps led to the third question mark in our diagram: "Is man an animal?" We even indicated the resistance that lived (and probably still lives) in many of us to acknowledging that man is an animal. As far as the attitude of orthodox science is concerned, however, the question mark in our diagram after animal must be replaced now by a note of exclamation! The expression, "Man is an animal" (we are reminded of the book, *The Naked Ape* by Desmond Morris), includes more than merely biological and anthropological terminology. Connected with it is something not often recognized: the conviction that man's existence is limited by birth and death.

Let us not forget that as long as man still had some connection with a spiritual world, be it only in the form of belief, and even if man did not pay much attention to a life before and after death, we can say that the spiritual world was at least experienced or considered as a reality. Birth and death were, for many people, still gates through which one could pass. We should try to feel the difference between "dying" and "passing away." In announcements of death we still experience belief and confidence in some sort of reality existing after death. As soon as we touch upon exact science, however, which claims more or less to possess the right conception of reality, life is considered to end at the moment of death, and it is obvious that we meet the same attitude toward life before birth.

We can enlarge our diagram as follows:

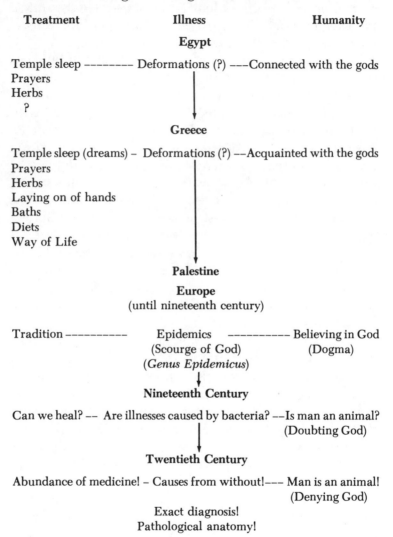

Treatment	Illness	Humanity

Egypt

Temple sleep ———————— Deformations (?) ———Connected with the gods
Prayers
Herbs
 ?

Greece

Temple sleep (dreams) – Deformations (?) ——Acquainted with the gods
Prayers
Herbs
Laying on of hands
Baths
Diets
Way of Life

Palestine

Europe
(until nineteenth century)

Tradition ——————— Epidemics ——————— Believing in God
(Scourge of God) (Dogma)
(*Genus Epidemicus*)

Nineteenth Century

Can we heal? —— Are illnesses caused by bacteria? ——Is man an animal?
(Doubting God)

Twentieth Century

Abundance of medicine! – Causes from without!——— Man is an animal!
(Denying God)
Exact diagnosis!
Pathological anatomy!

What follows now should not be looked upon as a lack of appreciation, nor should it be considered as willful contradiction or light-hearted criticism. One who is a little acquainted with the way medicines nowadays have come to be prescribed, promoted, or advertised, albeit mainly in medical periodicals, discovers an unexpected power in the field of medicine that has nothing to do with medicine at all but nevertheless has penetrated it with incredible force. This is the power of *economics*. Not every doctor is aware of the extent to which economics penetrates the medical sphere and how insidious its influence is.

How about the causes of illness? We have mentioned, for instance, chemical, physical, biological causes, but the question could arise: what eventually determines the chances of falling ill due to influences to which we are all exposed? We are met with the answer that it is a matter of *statistics!*

When we spoke about the Egyptian times, it was suggested that illness was based on some sort of deformation caused by man's way of life. In the times of the great epidemics these illnesses were called, not without reason, the "scourge of God." This again expresses the relationship between man's way of life and his health. Even when the cause of epidemics was attributed to the influence of the *genus epidemicus*, we still felt the influence of an unseen world. Isn't it interesting that this was generally accepted, right up into the first half of the nineteenth century.

What a difference when humanity is suddenly confronted with a conception saying the exact opposite. Together with the idea of "no watchmaker," no Creator, we meet the belief that illnesses are but a matter of chance. Our knowledge of the causes of illness is governed by the world of statistics, as economy threatens to take possession of the world of medicines. Moreover, the influence of statistics has become dominant in the application of medicine as well. Whether a medicine is useful or not is decided by experiments and statistics. We see the drastic change in man's approach to the world, culminating in the conclusion that man is an animal.

In many ways, psychologists have tried to illustrate the bestial character of man. They have described man as a bundle of desires, lusts and passions, sexual desires, nutritional desires, desire for power, etc. In spite of the fact that I personally think that in this consideration the essence of the human being is forgotten, we cannot deny that many animal qualities are found in the human soul. To conclude, however, that man is an animal must create a different attitude toward humanity. In my book, *The Dressed Angel*, I tried to show that a great proportion of the phenomena in modern medical treatment, in modern education, and in modern social life itself can be brought back to the fact that we have lost touch with the human element in humanity. This is one of the reasons that the expression, "Man is an animal," has been replaced by the impression that many of us may have received, especially in clinics, that man is merely a *number*. Is it not so that in many ways, in many fields of daily life, man has become a number? Is it not the aim of our society to give everyone his own number? Though there are practical reasons for this that we can accept, we should be aware of the connection between economy, statistics, and number. If we put these things together, it is as if we suddenly recognize an unexpected element in the situation that we are analyzing. This element shows itself in these three words. I do not mean the words as such but the principle that is circumscribed by these words. We will elaborate on this subject later and even find another expression for it. In the meantime, there is one more point to consider.

Why has medicine lost its interest in herbs? Why is the idea that illnesses have some relationship to a "higher world" rejected? Why is man degraded to an animal-like being? Why this aversion to any divine element? It is almost surprising how often the word "herb" evokes the thought of a quack doctor. As soon as we analyze the plant substance and look for the active element in it, as soon as we enter the science of biochemistry, we are supposed to be scientists. Here too, however, we must confess that we have lost sight of the plant as a whole. We have lifted the plant out of its natural environment, which means out of the situation where we still meet it as a creation of God. In short, even the herbs still remind us of the divine essence, whereas what was indicated above presents itself more and more in opposition to the divine element.

Contemplating once more the question marks in our diagram, taking into account the great transition to the three expressions followed by exclamation marks, we find a sequence. The exuberance, certainty, and pride of our time follow a time of hesitation. We should put arrows into our diagram, indicating the shift from hesitation to certainty, pointing from our row of question marks to the next stage of development. On the other side, we have spoken about economics, statistics, and number and the influences of forces penetrating the field of modern medical science with incredible intensity. Here, we have arrows pointing in the opposite direction.

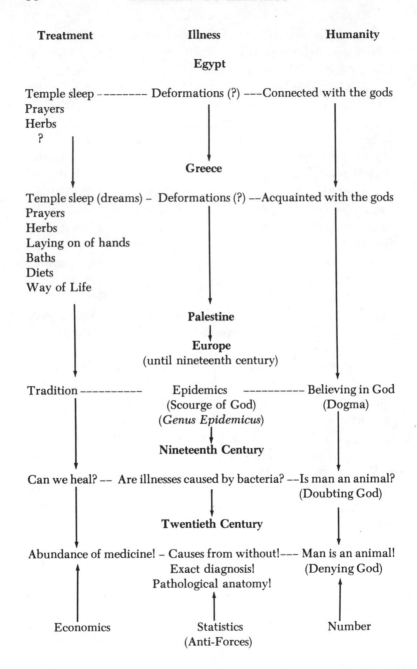

Treatment   **Illness**   **Humanity**

Egypt

Temple sleep --------- Deformations (?) ---Connected with the gods
Prayers
Herbs
 ?

Greece

Temple sleep (dreams) - Deformations (?) --Acquainted with the gods
Prayers
Herbs
Laying on of hands
Baths
Diets
Way of Life

Palestine

Europe
(until nineteenth century)

Tradition ----------   Epidemics   ---------- Believing in God
                (Scourge of God)   (Dogma)
                (*Genus Epidemicus*)

Nineteenth Century

Can we heal? -- Are illnesses caused by bacteria? --Is man an animal?
                                     (Doubting God)

Twentieth Century

Abundance of medicine! - Causes from without!--- Man is an animal!
                Exact diagnosis!   (Denying God)
              Pathological anatomy!

Economics   Statistics   Number
                (Anti-Forces)

Though I hesitate to do so, I would like to make one last comment here. The fact cannot be denied that economics, which in itself is something circumscribed and correct, evokes the pursuit of gain; that statistics, which in itself is something circumscribed and correct, evokes a lie (a well-known illustration is the expression, "I believe a statistic only if I have falsified it myself"); and that the result of treating man as a number is a lack of respect for our fellow men. I said that I hesitate to say this, because I know all too well that such a suggestion is easily considered an effort to disqualify modern medicine, to create a negative atmosphere. Out of what has been said just before it may be clear that we have to do with experiences that must be seen and can be judged in the proper way only if we look from afar at the whole of medical history.

I am well aware of the fact that I have created a certain atmosphere around the field of medicine that could be called confusing. Let us not forget, however, that while we can recognize, measure, and restore irregularities in the human body to an extent many of us would never have dreamt of some ten years ago, we have also learned about doubts and disappointments. Let us, by all means, not forget the beginning of this book, the article by Jongkees, asking for the reasons for these doubts and misgivings.

One of the rules still valid when I began my medical studies was "*primum nil nocere*" (above all, no harm should be done). What a difference compared with the present, in which there has been a threatening increase in iatrogenic illnesses.* Official medicine estimates that more than 15% of patients in clinics are ill because of their medicine and their treatments. The man in the street hears these rumors; he has his own experiences of

---

*Illness caused by the treatment of doctors.

being treated as a number, of being stuffed with medicines and confronted with their often unfavorable effects; he therefore looks toward what are called "alternative treatments." It makes little sense to fight these treatments, as we should not try to indoctrinate anyone with our conceptions and convictions.

Many people, doctors no less than others, have left the path of orthodox medicine. Naturopathy, homeopathy, acupuncture, and so on are coming into prominence. An increasing number of patients who have lost confidence in "normal" medicine seek help and comfort by these means. We may also mention the great number of magnetists, radioesthesists, herbalists, iroscopists, and so forth. Furthermore, we know of medical books in which doctors state that medicine has gone totally astray. These doctors have not chosen any of the mentioned alternative treatments but are, for the moment, criticizing the situation in modern clinics, pharmacies, and so forth. Many people are awake to the feeling that "something is wrong."

I have touched on the expression "alternative medicine" to stress my attitude in this respect. I firmly believe that we should not leave the realm of official medicine. Besides, many forms of alternative medicine are, in my experience, based on tradition. We find the same problem when we see people who no longer can stand the materialistic thinking of our time and flee back to Oriental world conceptions. We could perhaps characterize this movement as "fleeing exactness," fleeing the world of differentiation and rejecting the achievements of the last centuries at the same time. Personally, I cannot agree with this attitude. On the contrary, I am convinced that we can and must introduce into medicine, also into modern orthodox medicine, a new way of thinking, so that ancient values are reborn in the world of differentiation and so that we can develop a totally new view of humanity and life on earth, of illness, of treatment and healing. Instead of alternative medicine, we may introduce the term the "extension of medicine."

IV

Toward an Extension of Modern Medicine

A Conversation

To begin a new approach to medical treatment, I would like to refer to an interesting conversation I had during the second World War with a colleague whom I had not met beforehand. In speaking about illnesses and healing, I began to elaborate on the fact that modern medicine was discovering an increasing number of "deformations" in the human body. "By the word deformation I do not mean merely tumors, distorted joints, ulcers, abscesses, inflammations, and so on, but also high blood pressure, abnormal blood composition, and other such maladies." I pointed out that modern medicine was more and more capable of combating these traceable deformations. We might call this symptomatic treatment. I then applied this concept "symptomatic" to the example of a tumor, saying that we could, in a different sense, consider a tumor as a symptom of the illness cancer. In response to his question of what I meant by describing the tumor as a symptom, as opposed to the more common description of the tumor as an illness, I gave him the following answer: "The causes of illness may be summarized as chemical, physical, biological, psychological, and hereditary. However," I continued, "the riddle remains when, under the same circumstances, certain people will fall ill, while others will not. We should thus add a sixth element as a condition for falling ill: the predisposition."

He could easily follow what I was saying and only asked where I thought the site of the predisposition likely to be. "Here," I told him, "we find a great lack in modern science as far as living beings are concerned, especially the human being. In spite of our materialistic times, we are allowed to speak of the soul. Psychologists deal with the reality of the human soul, apart from possible theories about the origin of the soul. The soul is a recognized principle.

"We come across the same when speaking of the spirit. Priests and philosophers use the word 'spirit' as a reality, which is more or less distinguished from the soul. There is, however, a third principle that we cannot and should not ignore: life as a reality in itself.*

"Life is generally considered to be a function of the physical, biochemical construction. Yet to find a new approach toward life as a reality, we should ask not only what the cause of illness is but perhaps the more important question, what is the cause of healing?"

I was pointing to something quite obvious, which everyone is aware of through his own experience, for instance, the healing of a wound. I continued: "What we should marvel at is the restoration of the form! When we ask a doctor who is firmly convinced that matter is the only reality how a form can be restored (a daily occurrence in the field of surgery and medicine), generally his answer will be: the *"vis medicatrix naturae,"* the natural healing force. It goes without saying that this is nothing

---

*This has also been mentioned in the description of healing through temple sleep in Egypt.

more than an evasion and an admission that we do not know; it is a question mark.

"We can extend our knowledge and comprehension of these restoring forces by looking at the living being, man, from birth till death. We cannot but marvel at the fact that the human body is maintained in its 'form' during its whole life, and also during sleep, falling apart only at the moment of death. The conclusion is simple: some sort of forces are maintaining the form of our body during life, forces that at the same time are able to restore a deformation if the circumstances are favorable. These forces could be called the 'formative forces,' or the 'body of formative forces,' or the 'body of life-forces,' or the 'life-body.' In early times, man generally spoke of the 'etheric body.' It is of little importance what we call it.

"So, death is marked by the moment when the life-body withdraws itself from the physical body. The physical body then becomes subject to the laws of dead nature. We could call this 'decomposition' in contrast to the expression 'composition,' which is manifest in the building up of the human form during our lifetime. It is important to mention the fact that this conception forces us to change our view concerning the essence of matter. Matter in a living body is not the same as matter in the mineral world. The best way to explain this is by saying that it changes its 'orientation.' The substances are united in a oneness consisting of the aforementioned life-body or body of formative forces. Living substance is not a highly complicated compound of particles but a fully new *continuum*, which is the substance of the living form in plant, animal, and man. Besides, in animal and man this form appears changed by the additional influence of soul and spirit.

"It is clear, however, that spirit, soul, and life can be

seen, experienced, and can exist on earth only because the mineral kingdom permeates them."

My colleague, being a religious man, could still quite agree. He had no problem accepting an invisible reality, the effect and results of which he could see in the visible world. I then continued: "The fact that the five causes of illness I mentioned need a predisposition to produce an illness can be expressed in this way: an illness is the visibility of a predisposition. However, as illness is a deformation of the physical body, and the form of the physical body is the result of the activity of the body of formative forces or the life-body, we can conclude that the predisposition is a deformation in that same life-body.*

"If we consider the consequence of the idea of a pre-disposition, we come to understand that an illness can never appear in a healthy body. We could say it the other way around: a healthy person can never fall ill, i.e., there must already be some predisposition that we generally come to know only in the moment someone falls ill.**

"This conclusion is often challenged by saying that, in the case of a town of some 300,000 people invaded by an epidemic of some sort, e.g., cholera, if 200,000 people fall ill, this would be a clear proof that it is not a question of predisposition but simply an attack from without. The answer to this objection is equally straightforward: what about the 100,000 people who did *not* fall ill? Certainly,

---

*The attentive reader may easily understand that here we come upon the same concept of deformation as was referred to regarding the Egyptian era.
**This statement is, of course, essential. The human body has a natural vulnerability, which should not confuse us. Influences from without may attack and damage a body without any predisposition, but here we enter into the realm of accidents. To say that a really healthy person never falls ill should be qualified by saying, "In the sense in which I am speaking."

the problem of epidemics is a problem of its own, which we will go into later. On the other hand, we can solve this problem by saying that it is only a matter of resistance. Later I will show that this is definitely incorrect.

"The predisposition is one of the reasons that on removing a tumor, we have done only half the work. Many think that the patient will be healed when the tumor is removed. A doctor who has experience in this field knows better. I may even state here that the increase in cancer may be due not only to ecological circumstances but also to changes in the actual human constitution. A real healing would come about only through treating the human life-body in such a way that we would be able to restore the deformation in that life-body, in other words, heal the predisposition.

Then it was his turn to enter the discussion. "Here lies the limit," he said. "To me, man's body is a creation of God. When you speak about creating forces, which, you say, belong to the life-body, I call this an illustration of God's creation of our body. Don't forget, however, that the sum of these creating forces, which in the first line of Genesis is called 'God,' and in the Gospel of St. John is called the "Word," is principally God's activity. To speak of "healing the predisposition," in the sense you have explained, would mean nothing less than joining the Creator in His activity. This is what I must call heresy. Are you so audacious as to pretend that you could join in His creation or, to put it in other words, that you are able to speak the language of God?"

His point was to show me the limit of our capacities, and thus he was highly surprised when I told him that I dared to say that I thought I knew where one could learn the language of God's creating forces. "Where?" he asked. My answer was, "In the kingdom of the plants."

The reader will be aware that, in speaking about pre-disposition and deformation, I have used expressions which, as we have shown, have come down to us through tradition out of a time in which the human being still had experiences of higher worlds that have gradually faded. We have called the predisposition a deformation in the life-body, using the same term that we used when we spoke about illness in the Egyptian and Greek periods. In both eras, we also came upon treatments with plants. The knowledge of these plants, however, was gained not by external investigations, as we would and could do now, but by an intuitive capacity. People "dreamt" of the plants, or at least visualized them, in a way appropriate to a consciousness that has been lost over the course of time.

With Paracelsus, as we have seen, a new approach to the kingdom of plants arose. He spoke about passing the examination of nature (in German, *"durch der Natur Examen gehen"*). He taught his pupils to look at the plants in a new way, to recognize their construction, to compare this construction with that of the human body and then try to come to the right application. Whether he succeeded or not is not important for the moment. The main point is that we can recognize in Paracelsus a pioneer in the same thoughts that I brought forward in the conversation with my colleague, which will be developed more extensively in the following chapters. For the moment, the main point is to begin a new direction in our investigations.

I would like to refer to an earlier remark about the Dutch herbalist, Mellie Uijldert, who wrote about the language of the herbs. I said that there were people all over the world who had an inkling of the relationship existing between plant forms and the form of the human body. It is evident, however, that the expression "language of the herbs" needs further clarification. In everyday thinking, we imagine the substance of a plant to work in a biochemical way on the substance of the human body. Because the body of formative forces, the life-body, is fully denied, the experience with homeopathic dilutions must be denied as well. If a modern doctor states—and it is always said in this way—that homeopathic dilutions can never have any effect, because in these higher dilutions we might find only one molecule of the substance in a glass of water, he is quite correct, if he is convinced that the dilution consists of a dispersion of molecules.

The plant, however, does not consist of molecules, and neither does man's body. A plant does not *consist* of matter but is *visible* through matter, and so is the human body. The invisible element shows itself in the "form," the particular construction of plant and man. When I dilute an herbal substance, it is as if I disperse a form, as if I release a form from its "enchantment." It is as if I am freeing the creating forces, the true being, "the truth" of the plant, from its physical imprisonment, thus enriching the diluting medium with it.

Returning to the idea of the life-body, we thus have, in homeopathic applications, nothing to do with the influence of substance on substance but with formative forces on formative forces, with the "Word on the Word." The concept of the life-body helps us to understand how the body listens to the language of a given medicine, which is also—in its essence—"form." What is given in the dilution is not easy to grasp with materialistic thinking, but rather than ignoring it, we should try to develop this thinking. We should try to become malleable, open to new ideas, which appeal not only to our heads but to the entire human being.

Often, in speaking to a large audience, I have had occasion to touch on the surprisingly strong effect of weak forces. Speaking about healing with homeopathic dilutions, I have asked the audience whether I might give an example of how one could lift several thousand kilograms with minimal force. It was agreed to let me give that illustration. I then begged the audience to stand for a moment. Everyone got up, but in rising, half the audience started laughing, until a roar of laughter filled the hall. A few words had sufficed to bring about an extraordinary physical effect. Then somebody remarked, "You have not lifted us; we stood by ourselves." "Quite correct," I replied, "but the same happens in the human body in the case of restoration of a form. The dilutions themselves are not restoring; what is restoring is the 'truth' of the plant form, which is living in the dilution and speaks its language to a human life-body that is inclined to listen to it."

In this way we understand the principle of healing more and more as a *restoration of the form.* This was also the result of healing in the Egyptian age, as has been pointed out already. Later we will understand that the healing forces in those treatments are closely related to those very forces out of which the plant has been created.

We described the effect of the restoration in the temple sleep as a possibility for man to continue his development, his evolution, his way. There is a great difference between the description of healing as "getting rid of the symptoms" and as "an annihilation of deformations" that prevent us from living and developing in the appropriate way in our body. We live with our spirit and our soul in our body, but this body is not a purely physical one; it is a form, a living form, kept together and maintained by invisible spiritual forces, which we have described as and referred to as the reality of life. Without reintroducing the principle of this reality in our conception of man, we will never be able to understand how spirit and soul can live in our body. Many doctors still doubt the reality of the soul. One of their main objections is, how could the soul, if such a non-physical element exists at all, be connected to a physical body? I think their objection is quite reasonable. If we consider our body as a purely material being, there is no link between soul and body, at least not as something we can imagine. Recognizing the reality of the life-body, the body of formative forces, however, creates just such a link. In this way, understanding that "man can again continue his evolution" creates the possibility of recognizing the link between the human in man and the divine, the spiritual world, which has been "lost from sight." In the next sections we will elaborate on this conclusion.

An additional remark will amplify the experiment of getting the audience to stand. If I had spoken in a foreign tongue, which the audience could not understand, nothing would have happened. Comparing this to the influence of medicine, one could say that I had given the wrong medicine. I could also have shouted a command to get up. In our comparison, this would have meant that I had given an unnecessarily large dose: unnecessary, because shouting or speaking normally would have produced the same effect. This also helps us to understand the difference between homeopathic and allopathic medicine. One aspirin has a certain effect; generally, two aspirins have twice that effect. Here the quantities play quite a different role from that in the world of homeopathic dilutions.

A New Impulse in Medicine

Let me explain why I have expressed myself sometimes in a perhaps unconventional manner. I have used

the word *life*-body or life-force purposely to show that
the reality of "life" must be visualized again. I have
spoken about the disenchantment of the plant form in the
dilutions, of the freeing of the *"truth"* from the plant.
Finally, we have tried to restore the instrinsic significance
of the word "evolution," hoping that this word will begin
to knock at the closed doors of birth and death. I spoke,
therefore, about evolution as going along a path, a *way*. I
have brought these three new expressions—life, truth,
and way—in connection with a renewal of medicine. The
question of which impulse should work in this renewal of
medicine can now be answered in a subtle way when we
remind ourselves of the words, spoken nearly 2,000 years
ago by Christ, "I am the way, the truth, and the life."

In the description of the Greek era, we spoke of the
hidden impulse of Christ's activity in the field of medicine
and noted that, in the development of orthodox medicine,
this impulse has not had the slightest influence. I even said
that it had to wait for its time. Perhaps the time has come.
Perhaps we have come to those limits that threaten
humanity. Perhaps we have come to the point where
man's evolution is in danger of being blocked. Deterioration, blockage—both are words meant to express the
manifold feelings that more and more are being brought to
the fore throughout the world of medicine today.

In the following, it will be our task to determine
whether or not we have the right to speak of a new impulse in our evolution in such a way as has been indicated. Before we can attempt this, however, another
problem stands before us. We have gradually done away
with the concepts of "way," "truth," and "life"—as we
have shown in the present-day description of man as an
animal, of illnesses as attacks on man from without (more
or less at random), and of the treatment of illnesses as

eliminating physical deformations, which we have called symptoms. Such a state of affairs may reveal an impulse contrary to the impulse we called the Christian one. Is this merely an abstract idea, or does this thought indeed point to a reality? If the latter is the case, from where does this negative impulse come? Let us, in the following, try to give a picture of modern medicine in such a way that this latter impulse is revealed with the necessary clarity. To me, this is of the greatest importance. Many people fight for the reality of the divine, for the acknowledgement of Christ. Should one not also begin, however, to be aware of anti-forces? I know quite well that even in the realm of religion and belief, this word is seldom used. Here and there you might hear the word "devil" mentioned, but rarely in all seriousness.

Perhaps I may show a special consequence here. If there were a God, and people denied Him, it is quite understandable that He would "feel sad." If, on the other hand, there were a devil, and people denied him, it is equally understandable that he would be "very glad"! It is as if people tend to turn their heads away from this question. It is ever so important to be able to differentiate in this realm of darkness, just as we try to do in the world of light. We must realize that the right characterization of the problematic elements in our lives creates at the same time the possibility of learning what these elements really are so that we can determine our attitude toward them.

Anti-Forces

We have pointed to the abundance of medicines that have been invented, discovered, and produced in the last forty to fifty years. The purpose of these medicines is to relieve ailments, to fight symptoms, symptoms being the visible disturbance, the physical nuisance. Today, we wish to rid ourselves of the complaints that prevent us from living the life offered by modern civilization and technology. Illness is of no use, of no sense, in such a life. We have already expressed this attitude in the phrase, "illness should not be." It is obvious that such a comment is closely related to the conception that human existence is limited by birth and death.

Along with this first approach to illness (the annihilation of symptoms and complaints), modern medicine has also introduced two treatments underlining the fact that today we look at life between birth and death as the only reality. These two treatments are the birth control pill and organ transplants.

I should like first of all to say a few words about transplants. In the animal kingdom, there is no problem regarding transplants—if we stick to the same species of animal. Humanity, however, has become so individualized that one could say that each person is a species of his own. Apart from rare exceptions (identical twins), transplants are impossible without special measures. These consist of the application of substances that suppress the so-called human immunity, "immunity suppressors." Our immunity, however, is an expression of our health, of that wonderful power of "maintenance" that creates and restores our shape or form. These *immuno-suppressiva* work to prevent the body from rejecting the transplanted organ.

I do not intend merely to draw attention to the unfavorable results of organ transplants but rather to correct the illusions that exist. Many of us will remember the first celebrated heart transplant operation performed by Dr. Barnard on Mr. Blaiberg in South Africa. The world was excited by the news of the success of this transplant, as rumors went around that after the operation, Blaiberg led a very exuberant life, sunbathing on the beach and swimming in the sea; in short, he was able, once again, fully to enjoy life. A short while after this miracle of medicine happened I practiced for a short period in South Africa, and I had the chance to meet one of Blaiberg's nurses. She said, "For the greater part of the 600 days he outlived the operation, Blaiberg was in bed. He had to take 100-150 tablets daily to prevent his new heart from being rejected. I have rarely in my life seen such a sick person, someone who felt so miserable." There may have been, indeed, a few days when he felt better and was driven by car to the beach, where he stood for a short while in the sun, momentarily even enjoying it perhaps. In any case, reporters from all sides came and made dozens of photographs that seem to verify the above rumor. I think it worthwhile to learn the truth about this, though the things I have said do not detract from the fact that the achievement itself can also be admired.

At that time, the practice of transplants, especially of organs, extended quickly over the whole civilized world. Many of us will still remember the atmosphere of excitement when a new success was achieved, if only for a short time. People began to expect a new era to come, in which transplants would play a very important role. Because of the unfavorable effects of the immuno-suppressors, however, the initial enthusiasm gradually faded. It has grown silent around the subject of transplants, though special forms are still in use and medicine is still trying and hoping for better times and methods. We could ask, however, if these substances have such a disturbing influence on our constitution, and if these effects obviously cannot be avoided, why are doctors so keen on continuing in their efforts? I think the reason for this is that in the course of time man is developing a special attitude toward the problem of death. It is as if we can almost hear the unspoken conviction, "Anything is allowed, if only one does not die, for after death, there is nothing at all." We should not forget, however, that transplants, while working according to our wishes, subtly intensify our fear of death at the same time.

How can we justify such a conviction? The answer is, because of the belief that existence stops at death. In the same way, we can begin to understand the attitude toward the problem of euthanasia. Transplants mean lengthening life; euthanasia means shortening life. Where does the synthesis lie? Considering euthanasia, we must not concern ourselves with euthanasia itself as a treatment but with the attitude toward euthanasia as a method. I think we cannot avoid considering the use of euthanasia, not only in cases of unbearable suffering but also, more and more, in cases of so-called senseless lives. The attitude would be—one might predict—"What does it matter if one cuts short an existence that will soon be ended anyhow?" If we are convinced that after death there is "nothing," there is no real objection to euthanasia in any proposed case! We can understand how this attitude toward euthanasia, just like the striving for lengthened life with transplants, can be seen as a consequence of the conviction that death is the limit of human existence.

In abortion we meet a similar problem. Abortion has quite a remarkable "predecessor," the Pill. Not the Pill as used to prevent conception but the Pill as a means of preventing the population explosion. The population explosion suggests that if one did not take the Pill humans would multiply like rabbits. This implies that man is an animal, which supports the view that life is limited be-

tween birth and death. This is not declared openly; perhaps it is not even intended. It is certainly a hidden suggestion, however, which can hardly be denied and has
had its consequences. It is not difficult to feel that the
changing attitude toward abortion can be seen as a direct
consequence of the conviction that before birth there is
nothing. Why need one be concerned about destroying
something that shortly before did not exist at all? If one is
convinced that existence starts at birth, the logic behind
abortions is perfect.* Hence the cry for unlimited abortion and the wish for unlimited numbers of transplants. It
is not important whether we still meet a lot of resistance
toward unlimited abortion or not, nor whether we have
succeeded in our wishes regarding transplants. What is
essential is the attitude toward life that lies behind both
phenomena.

These two examples underline, with increasing conviction, the fact that birth and death are no longer gates
but impermeable walls. In between, man leads his life,
supported by the ideal that illness should not be.

Illness should not be

Birth	Death
Beginning of existence	*End of existence*

I trust the foregoing line of thinking will help one to
understand this diagram clearly. We have pointed out
time and again that man's consciousness of the world,
beyond the limit of the world of the senses, has waned
and then disappeared. It has been shown that a serious
consideration of what has happened in the field of medi-

---

*In this respect it makes no difference whether we speak about life beginning at
birth or beginning at conception.

cine in the course of time generally can awaken a new awareness. If we imagine for a moment that life before birth and after death is still a reality, that man has an existence before birth and after death, then birth and death are considered gates again. Man can be seen as an individuality who leads his life on earth between these two gates. This creates an opportunity to look at illness again as part of his life.

What does the diagram suggest? The three lines indicate the barriers that imprison man's eternal being in the modern conceptions of a limited life on earth. The left vertical line stands for "Thou shalt not be born"; the right vertical line stands for "Thou shalt not die"; in between we "hear," "Thou shalt not suffer."

Thou shalt not suffer

Thou shalt   Thou shalt
not be born   not die

The phrase, "Thou shalt not," also used in connection with modern healing, "Thou shalt not suffer," needs some explanation. In the section, "A Characteristic of Medicine in the Beginning of the Twentieth Century," a long list of medicines that have appeared in the last fifty years was presented. Generally, as has been said, the world of medicine feels proud of this achievement. There is, however, one quality that nearly all these medicines have in common: they are "violent."

When a patient takes a sleeping pill, the effect is known: he will fall asleep. Perhaps two or more tablets will be needed. This makes no difference; the main point is that one cannot prevent oneself from falling asleep. When we spoke about the effects of homeopathic medicines—referring to them as a language that was heard, or maybe not heard, by the life-body—we had to do with an influence that the body may "answer" or not, as if we offer the body the opportunity to say "yes" or "no." In essence, we are allowing the body to make its own decision. In the case of an allopathic medicine, there is no question of refusing; in this sense, one can use the word "violence." It is not difficult to recognize this violence everywhere in medicine and also in so many realms of treatment: cytostatics (given in cases of cancer, leukemia, etc.), suppressors of immunity (given, for example, in cases of transplants), cortisone and its compounds (well known for their unbelievable effect on rheumatic complaints) are—besides having their dramatic effects—extremely harmful and must be applied with the greatest care.

Everyone is acquainted with the dangers connected with X-ray treatment and the like. Such examples justify the use of the word "violence." They also illustrate the phrase "Thou shalt not suffer" in connection with treatment. Why are these three sentences, "Thou shalt not be born," "Thou shalt not suffer," and "Thou shalt not die" of such importance? If we think for a moment of the word "Nativity" (birth), of the word "Easter" (the death and resurrection of Christ), and of the nearly three years of Christ's life after the Baptism in the Jordan, which may be called the Passion (the sufferings), the verb "to suffer" acquires a new significance. We remember times in our own lives, times of sorrow and pain, which may have been important episodes, which we would not have wished to miss on any account, because we felt there was sense in it. Life has sense; it is not senseless but rather an episode on earth that is part of the whole of human evolution. Here again, we meet the concept of a "path."

People may object to the fact that I seem to justify my

opinion with words from the Bible. I must reject this
argument emphatically. We have looked at phenomena
in a new way, but the Bible is also a phenomenon. If
someone were to say that one must exclude the Bible as a
phenomenon because he doesn't believe in the Bible, this
means in reality that he believes the Bible has no meaning. Such people are trying to replace belief with the wish
to know. If one believes that the Bible has no meaning,
however, one still believes. To reject the contents of the
Bible indicates prejudice, dogma, an *unscientific* attitude. In the beginning of this book, I tried to characterize the appropriate attitude in these situations by
saying that we should never believe something but also
never *not* believe something. Simply look at it, consider
it, and take it as a phenomenon. We must recognize the
fact that the Bible exists. The example offered earlier,
which shed a new light on the story of the New Testament, may make more sense than it did before. We discover a new, perhaps unexpected, perspective; that is,
certain phenomena start to support one another.

The English language has a wonderful expression,
"something makes sense." Of course, by this expression
we generally mean, "it is sensible." To me, however, it
has yet another significance. If we practice the aforementioned way of looking for images—for phenomena can
build up an image—we develop a new capacity; we
develop a sort of a talent, an ability for looking in a new
way at the world around us. We begin to develop a new
"sense," not for the world of the ordinary senses but for a
world that reveals itself between the sense impressions.
Could this be the first recognition, the first new experience, of a spiritual world?

We spoke about the Christian element that may begin
to evoke new values in our thoughts about illness and

healing. The "Thou shalt not. . ." expressions can teach us to understand how these anti-forces may also be seen as anti-Christian forces in the deepest sense of the word. The whole problem in the field of medicine, which is the theme of our discussion, clearly points in this direction. The influence of economics, statistics, and number presents a picture of such an attack.

If we consult the diagram on page 79 again, in the third column we progress from "Connected with the gods," "Acquainted with the gods," "Believing in God," to "Is man an animal?" Then under the question mark, we have the exclamation mark: "Man is an animal!" This is the beginning of a new attitude: "Doubting God" and "Denying God." The consequence of this attitude is the picture of abundance, exactness, and certainty we see in medical science today. In the diagram this is expressed in the three arrows pointing upward, as if approaching this medical world from the other side. We have called this an attack. One could say that these anti-forces, these powers, could only intervene after man had separated himself from the so-called divine world. It is as if these forces have waited for their time to come.

We may remember that on page 102 we used a similar expression. We spoke of another impulse, the "Christ impulse," which also had to wait for its time. We could conclude that the time in which we live now is the time when both experiences meet.

In surveying this development, little is gained in reference to these anti-forces by saying that they should not be. We will see gradually the important role they have played in the development of medicine, in the path toward future healing, but it is necessary to recognize them; otherwise, we become their prey.

Reflecting on what has been said, an afterthought

may be added. If a person is convinced that the education in medicine given in the university is on the right track, if someone only sees small side-problems that are just a matter of time, just a matter of regulation, just technical problems, he will shrug his shoulders at everything that has been said until now. These thoughts are not meant to convince him, however; these considerations are meant for those who have questions, who are looking for a way out, who are experiencing an important problem and asking for a solution. We might express such a feeling by saying that the human in man is in danger.

The three fields that have been our object from the beginning—treatment, illness, and humanity—will now be treated in the light of an extended view of medicine. I think it is of great importance to stipulate that the question posed at the beginning of this book—"Are we on the right path?"—should not be answered by a mere "no." Even when I think that we must discover a new direction in the development of medicine, even when I have tried to explain that man gradually has forgotten about real healing and has specialized in fighting and conquering symptoms, we should not forget that "fighting and conquering symptoms" is an achievement of great importance in medical treatment, for which we cannot be sufficiently grateful. If, for instance, healing of cancer would in reality mean healing the predisposition, this does not mean that we should exclude surgery or similar symptomatic treatments. We should be aware that the illness, which we have started to consider as a positive element in evolution, has a life of its own. We will see later (Chapter V) that the appearance of a tumor may be due to the retreat of the constructive forces of the body. Once a tumor has appeared, it displays a vitality that may be described as "careless." The fact that cancer does not respect anatomical boundaries reveals a similar impression. Therefore, of course in combination with efforts to strive to heal the predisposition toward cancer itself, we often will be forced to remove the tumor. Maybe in the future we will develop a method which, in the case of cancer, will make surgery superfluous; for the moment, however, we must be sober and realistic.

Let me give an example. A patient was suffering from cancer. She was the secretary of a famous author, who had nearly finished a book on botany in Australia. Several treatments had been suggested to her. None of them could guarantee healing; her chances were small. Modern medicine dispenses a powerful medicine, however, the so-called cytostatics, substances that set bounds to the growth of tissues. In this case, the situation was that the doctor could more or less treat her with orthodox methods but was unable to make any prognosis. Little chance of recovery remained. "However," he said, "if I give you cytostatics, you may be almost sure to have two more years left to live, but count on no more." As she thought it her duty to finish the book, which would take her approximately two years, she chose the second possibility. When I visited her, she had just finished her work and was fully prepared to die. I think it is important to mention such an example; it is instructive and helps us to look at the problems from different angles. At the same time we feel how essential it is to make decisions that are entirely our own responsibility.

The same applies to corresponding cases in the field of inflammations. In spite of the polarity between inflammation and tumor, they have one thing in common: both are vital processes. The vitality of the inflammation is, so to speak, an extension of one's own vitality; the tumor's vitality is an alien one; both are inclined to exceed their limits. In cases of inflammation, moreover, it can become compulsory to stop the process in order to reduce the abundance of vitality. If, as we have stated, antibiotics have been misused, probably to a large extent, we should not reject the possibility of making use of them in appropriate cases. On the contrary, we must, at least for the moment, accept every possibility offered for treatment, of course in strict accord with our own choice and conviction in each case. Prescriptions and rules can be constructive, but we should never exclude personal initiative.

Dramatic examples of achievements accomplished in modern medicine are, for instance, the development of insulin and Vitamin B12. Before 1922 a young person who had diabetes could be kept alive only by maintaining a strict diet, which, if the illness proceeded, could not save his life. One can hardly imagine what it meant when suddenly people no longer needed to die of diabetes. The same applies to the use of Vitamin B12 (originally the effect was achieved with the help of liver substances, called Pernaemon; later Vitamin B12 could be isolated and produced the same effect), by which a severe illness that nearly always ended with death, pernicious anaemia, could be stopped. Because I have witnessed the introduction of both treatments, I know full well how surprised and grateful the medical world was for these new discoveries. It is true, insulin and Pernaemon perform no healing, but they allow a person to lead a normal life.

Finally, let me add a few words on X-rays and other radioactive treatments. On the one hand, everyone knows about the terribly destructive results of many of these treatments, of the bad effect on the condition of the blood (leukemia!); on the other hand, no one who is acquainted with this field of treatment will deny the many instances in which some form of radium treatment has saved a life. One may conclude never to be fanatic, not in any way. Fanaticism is one of the attitudes we often encounter in relation to so-called alternative treatments as well as in orthodox medical conceptions. We mentioned an example of this already, with the words "no watchmaker." In the field of medical treatment another slogan has threatened freedom in medicine. Some years ago (especially in Germany) a group of doctors tried to make a law that cancer be treated by knife and rays only ("*Stahl und Strahl*"), that no other treatment should be allowed. I think the secretary's story, as an example, speaks for itself.

V

Considering Healing in a New Light

The Illness: Illness and Predisposition

First of all, we must study the principle of the predisposition. The word predisposition has been mentioned
often. We have to elaborate on this concept more extensively, coming to understand it as a deformation of the
life-body. What does a deformation of the life-body mean
if such a body consists of forces and not of physical elements? In our day, ever since Virchow, we have become
accustomed to understanding deformation as something
physical. It will not be easy, therefore, to train ourselves
to develop a new idea concerning deformation as expressed
in the word predisposition. *

What do we know about the word predisposition,
how can we sum up its qualities? Let us think of scarlet
fever: either we have a predisposition toward it or we do
not. If we do, the predisposition may be strong or weak,
it may show itself early in life or late. By strong or weak,

---

*One could say that animals are also vulnerable to bacteria, bacilli, viruses, etc;
thus they also have a predisposition. This, however, is incorrect. A certain type
of animal, e.g., the white mouse, is sensitive to the pneumonia bacillus, without exception. One can better characterize the animal by saying that an
animal *has* no predisposition, an animal *is* a predisposition.

117

we mean that one person can suffer from high fever and show all typical symptoms to a high degree, while someone else will have only a temperature and a few symptoms. If the predisposition shows itself late in life, this could mean that someone has gone through an epidemic in his youth, without catching the illness, and that some ten or twenty years later there is another epidemic and he subsequently falls ill.

Another fact concerning predisposition is that we have a specific predisposition for a specific illness. This is an interesting problem; very often it is said that it is only a matter of resistance whether one catches an infection or not. This, however, leads us away from the facts. Whether one catches the measles or typhoid fever has not, in the first place, to do with resistance but with a specific predisposition. We might remind ourselves that in times of epidemics—here I may point to the flu epidemic in 1918—often the strong, young people are the victims. We can best compare the predisposition for an illness with a particular talent. While I may have a talent to be a musician, I need not necessarily have a talent for painting.

We come upon the same thing in the domain of sympathies, which draw people together and create relationships. We could even say, for instance, that we marry someone because we have a predisposition for him or her. We could also say that we develop ability as a violinist because we have a predisposition for the violin. Might we thus not also be able to speak of having a talent for an illness? Is it not more attractive to speak of having a talent for measles rather than a predisposition for it? Whatever one calls it, in cases of talents, abilities, or relationships we meet the possibilities of its existing or not, of its being weak or strong, early or late.

The problem of the individual talent (illness, profession, relationship) is one that also can be studied historically. In the course of time, talents, of whatever sort, have become more and more individualized. Speaking about art in ancient times, we often wonder how it is possible that everyone was capable of creating something beautiful. One gets the impression that the entire population was in a way artistic. The real *individual* artists appeared only in the Greek time.*

We can now understand better that, in the time of the temple healings, illnesses were also group-illnesses. In the course of time, as man became more individualized, the predispositions became more individual as well. The question that is asked so often, "Why must I have that illness, why not someone else?" is a most important one, which runs through our daily problems where illnesses are concerned and must be answered some time and in some way. We can recognize, however, that this question must also be studied from a historical perspective, as it has become such a problem of our times. In ancient times, people never considered illnesses as senseless. In the section, "A Characteristic of Medicine in the Beginning of the Twentieth Century," we showed that in those days there was still a form of fatalism in the minds of people regarding illness. This we could call a last remnant of an ancient knowledge that illness "belonged" to someone.

---

*This is one of the points at which we come upon the essential difference between man and animal. The specialties of an animal (in the section on Hippocrates we spoke of "cosmic wisdom" in connection with the spider) are always and fully inherited. I have mentioned the fact that psychologists often emphasize the animal-qualities of man, and I have agreed that these qualities cannot be denied. We may characterize the difference remaining between animal and man by saying that while man may have the qualities of a dog, the dog itself does not have the qualities of a dog but *is* a dog. Consequently we can say that the animal *has* no talents, the animal *is* a talent!

⌣⌣⌣ we not look forward to a future time when illness once again will be considered as "not senseless"?

What, then, is the *cause* of the deformation in the life-body? The original cause can only emerge from the life of the soul. In the soul of man we meet that principle which we have already considered in speaking about the origin of the deformation in the Egyptian era. We mentioned the expression "fall of man." It is clear that in this sense we can speak about illness only in connection with humanity. Plant diseases, animal illnesses have a totally different meaning. They can only come into being if there is something wrong in their environment. The plant "being" and the animal "being" can never have anything to do with the words "sin" or "evil."

To many readers, connecting illness with sin might be seen as something of the past, which we have finally overcome. I can quite well understand that the trend of development in medical science has led us away from any conception concerning a relationship between illness and morality. To conclude, however, that we have arrived at a point at which we could do away with ancient conceptions as prejudices is, I think, premature. Several times we have already seen that it is possible to gain a new approach to principles that come to us out of the past and may gradually appear in a new light, the light of thinking and differentiation.—We must understand, though, that the word "sin" stands for everything that disturbs the harmony of the soul, e.g., irritations, stress, or whatever.

To understand the real meaning of a predisposition in the life-body, we always must remind ourselves of the fact that such irregularities arise out of the psyche, the soul life. This soul life is built up of what we have called "soul" and "spirit"; in the soul lie feelings of sympathy and antipathy, feelings in general. This soul life in man is, during the daytime, permeated by the spirit, man's spiritual being, indicated by everything having to do with knowledge, recognition, and self-awareness. It is this element that makes man an individual. We could speak of the soul life as being that through which, as long as we are awake, the reality of a spiritual world continually sounds. The human being, as a soul being, can be called a "through-sounder"; the word "*per-son*" means exactly that. If the reader is acquainted with details of Greek drama, he may know that the actors wore masks called "*persona*": "through-sounders." This information makes it possible to discover a new secret in humanity's evolution. If today we are together with other people, we may have difficulties—and this is so often the case—in really meeting another person, in building up some real form of relationship. Some time ago, during a discussion, someone said, "In modern times, it is as if everyone carries his personality as a mask in front of himself, hiding his real being." I do not think such an impression need surprise us. This "wearing of a mask in front of us" is a typical symptom of being a personality, an *individuum*.

How was it with the Greek people, however? We have seen that certainly they were no longer the equal, sheep-like groups of thousands of years ago. Nor, however, were they already as individualized as humanity has become in our times. Does it not seem as if in Greek drama we encounter some sort of anticipation of future times? Does it not make sense to imagine that becoming an individual personality is a condition for human evolution? Such a thought would certainly reveal Greek drama as an instructive experiment that evoked the feeling of earnestness and awe we still admire so highly.

Continuing our discussion of predisposition and illness, we can say that, normally, spirit and soul have a harmonious, "breathing" connection with the living body, which creates in a healthy person the wonderful feeling of transparency ("through-appearing condition"). In the case of the origin of an illness (the predisposition), we have to do with the opposite: an irregular, unfavorable attachment between soul and life-body. We could say that the life-body is no longer completely transparent. This need not be considered purely locally; it is a complicated process, which, in connection with the character of the illness, finally manifests itself in a special place or system.

To summarize, we have defined the predisposition as a quality of the life-body, as a deformation in that life-body that becomes visible in an illness. To clarify this, I would like to make a comparison. Let us imagine a day of wonderfully bright weather, warm and sunny with a steady temperature, perhaps a little hazy, yet with a blue sky. On such days we often have a feeling of a healthy atmosphere, which may maintain itself for some time. In meteorology, especially in regions with mountains and valleys, we often speak about healthy, steady air-bodies with equal temperatures in the different layers of the air. Imagine that a cloud appears "out of the blue," as it were. Now, three things can happen. It could disappear again, "dissolved by the warmth"; one could say it was not able to maintain itself, that it was "conquered" by the environment. A second possibility is that it remains the same for some time, in equilibrium with the surrounding conditions. The third possibility is that it can grow larger and darker, eventually causing rain. The rain is the cloud itself. By this rain the cloud gives up its existence! But what makes the cloud rain? Influences from the earth, from its environment.

Here the comparison ends, but we might take up the possibility of disappearing in two ways: volatilization or raining down. The first possibility could be called a spontaneous healing of an unfavorable condition. The rain, on the other hand, may be considered as an image of a physical illness that also appears, so to speak, "out of the blue." This comparison allows us to understand that disturbances of the healthy condition of our life-body need not always lead to illness. From the same direction from which the psychic cause of the illness emerges may come a correcting influence as well. Everyone knows the favorable influences of a change in the soul life. (Perhaps here we find an acceptable approach to the principle of so-called psychic healings.)

I will not say that this is an illustration of the ancient, well-known expression that man, as a microcosm, is an image of the macrocosm, but if someone were to say so, I would not object. Maybe we should look increasingly for similar illustrations.

When speaking about the essence of the predisposition, it has been said already that we are in the realm of the non-exact world, and thus we must deal with laws that appear in a different way from those that are found in the purely physical world. The predisposition for an illness need not be specific from the beginning. When we think of a predisposition for the measles, the predisposition is specific only if we consider the situation a short time before the outbreak of the illness. Such a predisposition can, so to speak, become tangible in several ways, depending on the influence of the environment. It is only after a special and critical moment that the result becomes fixed: we can say that the relationship between body and environment grows "specific"!

We now come to a very important point, to the effect of the illness on the predisposition that originally had led to the illness. We have seen that the appearance of the illness is the result of a number of factors: on the one hand, of the predisposition, which needs perhaps a long time to become more or less fixed; on the other hand, of the environment with its external influences (page 93), mainly a combination of physical (chemical, physical, biological, hereditary) and psychic (psychosomatic) influences.

The influence of the illness on the previously existing predisposition is well known in the case of epidemic illnesses. We find examples in daily life in children's illnesses. If a child has had scarlet fever, chicken pox, whooping cough, or whatever, he has overcome the predisposition; the predisposition has disappeared. Nobody should object to this just because he may have witnessed a child having the measles twice; the only sensible answer to that would be that this special child needed such an illness twice to rid himself of the predisposition.

In the trend of modern thinking, we often encounter another description of what we have called a predisposition. If someone has overcome a contagious illness it is said that he has acquired immunity. If someone has no predisposition whatsoever, he has an inborn immunity. Predisposition, therefore, is often considered as lack of immunity. In this way we bring the principle of predisposition back to the problem of being immune or not, which, in turn, depends on biochemical conditions. It is as though we are not in need of introducing a principle of formative forces. I think that here lies the danger of an error in our thinking. We certainly cannot deny that predisposition may also produce differences in biochemistry, but this is only an illustration in the realm of the physical body. The question is: what are the forces that organize the whole of biochemistry, that we can investigate through our laboratory experiments? Matter never can organize itself; it undergoes organization. We meet the same error when people try to explain the phenomenon of heredity by attributing the organizing principle to a physical substrate, for instance, the DNA molecule. How often do we hear that this or that is ruled by the DNA molecule. As if a molecule could ever rule! What we do is simply push the problem back out of the field of vision. We find an illustration of this illusion in the statement, "the form of a living being, plant, animal, or man, is the result of its genetic structure." The first thing we must ask is from where the genetic structure itself comes.

I discussed a similar problem years ago when I met someone with whom I was musing over the relationship between thinking and activity of the brain. He said, "It is my brain that produces the thoughts," and indeed this is a conception generally acknowledged in physiology. To illustrate his statement, he continued, "If I damage my brain, I can no longer think properly." As he was a musician, I answered, "If I damage your piano, you can no longer play properly, but you would not conclude that it is the piano that has been playing. Similarly, if there is some damage to your brain you are no longer able to think, but it is nevertheless you who does the thinking, not your brain."

Continuing with our original problem, we can say that, in accepting the relationship between genetic structure and inherited form, we cannot assume that the form is the result of the genetic structure, but the genetic structure is the result of the source of activity that creates the form. That very activity creates a form in its totality, working into every element that we find as structure in every part of that form. We could even say that the creating element produces a form in all details, down to the smallest parts of the form, into the formula, the genetic structure.

I hope that it is clear that we shall never find a way out of these questions if we do not accept anew the reality of what already has been called a "spiritual being." A form itself is the creation of a spiritual being. Perhaps here we may add that form should not be confused with contour. Every physical form shows a contour, it is true, but a piece of rock, for instance, has *only* a contour and no form in the sense that the word is used here. In a form each part of its structure stands in special relationship to every other part of that structure, a relationship established by the composing being. The contour of a stone is the result of forces from without that have shaped it in connection with physical circumstances working, so to speak, at random.* We could express this conclusion in the following words: the body, as a physical being, can be looked at as composed *out* of matter; as a form it is composed *by* formative forces, forces that issue out of a being, a creating being.

We have developed so many prejudices in this field that we forget we are surrounded by the most obvious example of spiritual beings, humans. True, man has a physical body; when I touch him, he may even say, "that's me," but that is not true; it is his body only. If someone says, "I am John Smith," that is not true either; it is only his name. We meet the real being when we think of the center of man which *bears* a name and *has* a body. That center is invisible and yet the source of the human's creative capacities. Man should not forget that he is a creator; even the conception in which man denies that this is the case is one of his own creations.

Until now the expression life-body has been used as

---

*Where crystals are concerned, we have to do with special conditions which we cannot discuss here.

synonymous with "body of formative forces" and "etheric body." We meet the same principle in "the Archaeus" of Paracelsus, in "Prana" of the Orient, and in many other cases. Out of what has been said before, it follows that the human life-body must be quite different from that of an animal and that of a plant. The plant reveals the activity of formative forces in the purest form. The animal, being endowed with a soul, shows a totally different form, as his formative forces are organized by this new principle. The human body, again, is different from the animal one, as man's being is a revelation of a still higher principle, which we called spirit and which we can also call the "ego." The life-body, and consequently also the physical body of man, thus reveal an ego-organization. In the following we will, in special situations, use the expression ego-organization instead of life-body, meaning life-body organized by the ego.

Returning to the suggestion that illness takes away the predisposition, the question arises: is this always valid? If we shift now to other, non-epidemic illnesses, most people will hesitate to acknowledge a similar law, and yet I am convinced that the law always holds: *illness is the annihilation of the predisposition.*

We can find some interesting examples to bring this to light. If someone has an attack of migraine, we can ask why the attack of migraine occurs at that particular moment. Knowing a number of factors, we can summarize the problem by saying that different qualities of the patient and influences of his environment have, in the course of a certain period, brought into being a condition which, at a certain moment, explodes. The attack may last several hours, may even last some days. Everyone who has suffered from migraine will know what that means, but at the same time such a person will have experienced the wonderful relief when the attack comes to an end. We may call the attack of migraine the physical appearance that annihilates, for the time being, a condition that had been built up previously. We need not be concerned that someone may have had migraine attacks for several years; the principle of the law is not touched by that fact.

Of course, the greatest problem arises when we deal with chronic illnesses of which, so to speak, one never sees the end. These are illnesses that do not show the slightest tendency of healing. Here we will have great difficulty in coming to a similar conclusion. We will later see that the main principle of this experience is always relevant.

To go on, we must first of all ask ourselves: what is the *sense* of taking away the predisposition? Another story may illustrate this. In a village were two women leaning up against a fence, knitting and chatting away. One of them said to the other, "You know my little boy, John?" "Yes, I do." "I don't know what has come over him these days; he is intolerable. Do you know what I think?" "No," was the reply. "I'll tell you; I think it would do him a lot of good to get the measles." And then the boy did. Afterward he was a changed boy. I call the wisdom of these women—who wear aprons—"apron wisdom," and I think that much apron wisdom surpasses our university knowledge! In what way was the boy changed? His body "fit" him again. We have seen that the soul lives in the life-body, and we can imagine that if the life-body has a deformation, the soul cannot inhabit it properly.

A simple example of this can be experienced when we ask a person, "How do you do?" The answer may be, "I feel fine." Then we should ask him in return, "How do you know you feel fine?" The answer should be, "Because I don't feel anything." This expresses that wonderful feel-

ing of transparency that lives in us when we are healthy
and that has been referred to previously. In the example
above we can say that the measles took away the deformation in the life-body, allowing it again to be come
transparent. It was the same transparency that appeared
when the sky was clearing, as shown in our example on
page 122.

I am sure it has become clear how difficult it is to find
appropriate words to explain the problem of the predisposition in connection with illness. If we think of the
wealth of exact information we get from pathological
anatomy, a science that has been developed to an unbelievable extent during the last century, we might be inclined to stick to that information, hoping to find a real
explanation, grateful to find such an exactness. Already
in the section called "Introduction," I pointed out this
love for exactness that has played such a great role in the
development of modern science. In introducing the concept of formative forces, life-body, etc., a scientist can
have the feeling that he is losing firm ground of exact
knowledge, which he was glad to stand on, that he is
thrown into a realm of uncertainty again. I think it is a
very understandable complaint and at the same time a
very important turning point. In some way it is true that
we leave exactness and enter into the "inactness."* "Exact" means: out of the world of action, activity, creation.
The visible world is exact; that is why we are able to distinguish things so clearly. When, however, in continuing
our investigations we are forced to leave the firm ground
of exactness and enter the world of "inactness," we
become aware that *exact* also means *dead* and that the

---

*The word "inactness" will not be found in a dictionary. It is a consequence of
our exploration.

path of science in the course of time has led us from life to death. We could even say, however, that it has led from life to death to life again, for to the world of exactness we owe not only the necessary capacity for differentiating but also the capacity for entering anew the "inexact" world. We need not lose for a moment the ability to distinguish. In short, we reach again for the heights while, at the same time, remaining firmly on the ground.

Could it be that modern medical science itself is beginning to become aware that it cannot go on attaching itself solely to that world of exactitude? Could it be that this way will also lead us to the question, "Are we on the right path?"

To summarize, we have learned about the importance of the influence of the environment: chemical, physical, biological, psychological, and hereditary influences, all of which lead to bodily illness emerging out of the predisposition. When we hear that smoking causes cancer of the lungs, this is only part of the truth. A predisposition is a necessary precondition, though the devastating influence of smoking is clearly a known cause. We have understood that a predisposition does not always need to produce an illness. Illnesses may disappear by themselves, just as we said that a cloud may disappear without causing rain, if the conditions are favorable. On the other hand, we have seen that the appearance of an illness also offers a possibility for getting rid of a deforming predisposition. We could explain this last point in the words: *illness is the embodiment of a deformation that otherwise might inhibit human evolution.*

One may now feel that the slogan "illness should not be" expresses the exact opposite of these ideas. Is it not striking that we come to the opposite conclusion, that the possibility of falling ill is one of the greatest blessings in one's life? I am quite aware, however, that we must add many more arguments to support such a statement. I understand that one may respond to such a comment by asking, why then should a doctor practice at all? If all illnesses were just measles or chickenpox, I could even agree to some extent, but when we must deal with destructive illnesses like rheumatism, cancer, diseases of the central nervous system and of the heart and vessels, and so on, all of them predispositions made visible and for which the aforementioned law, "Illness takes away the predisposition," is valid, my answer would be, just as the patient does not accept these illnesses, I too will not accept these illnesses as such. Why? I do not think it is easy to give a rational answer to this question. In man lives the spontaneous wish to help. Here we may be reminded of the conversation I described regarding the appropriate treatment of the predisposition (see page 93). If an illness, for instance a tumor, eliminates, as we have said, the predisposition, and if I wish to rid myself of the tumor, I must take over its task, which means that I must annihilate the predisposition, so that the tumor does not have to do it. Here, for the first time, we come upon a word that I have described as gradually having lost its original meaning, the word "healing." Doing away with the symptoms of an illness is not healing; it is merely supporting the spontaneous restoration. "Annihilation" of the predisposition through an illness is, on the contrary, healing, though it happens without man's interference.

We have the expression, to "recover" from an illness. Is this not an interesting expression, to recover? The cover or, in other words, the living body in which I live, has become another cover, has undergone a restoration. The deformation has been annihilated! On the other hand, I would like, when speaking of healing, to limit the expres-

sion to the specific activity of a being who heals. Thinking back to the old Egyptian era, we could say that man
was being "recovered" by the healing of the gods.

If man himself is to undertake that activity to which I
have referred as "taking over the task of an illness"—we
spoke just now about a tumor—we encounter the same
situation. We can distinguish between the restoration or
the recovery and the activity that has brought this restoration into being. This means that what has once been
performed by the healing beings must now be taken over
by man himself, particularly in cases of destructive illnesses such as cancer, for instance. Here, the human being must enter into an activity that is not done by nature
but by himself alone. Restoration through an illness happens through nature. Healing by man is based on his *will*
for helping, his *will* for healing. It originates in an individual; healing is "original." We will see how the different elements that already have been indicated in the field
of healing will merge, until a wonderful conclusion
arises. To be able fully to appreciate this result, however,
we first must consider a number of other problems.

Inflammation and Cancer: a Polarity

We have discovered that illness can show two totally
different aspects. One group of illnesses comes under the
heading of inflammations. These illnesses appear and disappear, can even disappear by themselves. The clearest
example of an inflammation is an infectious epidemic illness. A patient with a high fever is "in flames," he is red
and warm; he perspires and has a quick pulse and quick
respiration. What impression does this give us? First of
all, we see great activity. We encounter the same picture
when we see a healthy person exert himself in heavy
labor. True, in this case, *he* is full of activity; in the sick

body, something else is active, and we must ask ourselves, *what* is active in case of a fever?

To find the answer we must look at the result of the activity. We have seen that the result is the disappearance of the predisposition, of the deformation, or, as we said, the restoration of the form. The form, however, was the result of the activity of the formative forces. What, then, is the consequence of this thought? It is common knowledge that maintenance of our body is performed by forces that require warmth for their activity. Our daily warmth is therefore a condition; our daily warmth allows us to be healthy. "You look well," is an expression meant to indicate a person's color, the wonderful coloring, which in the world of painting has typically been called *incarnate!* We are incarnated in the right way if we are in possession of the proper warmth-organization; our warmth-organization is the basis of our health. In the case of a fever this warmth increases. The activity of our formative forces not only maintains but restores our form.

It has been shown that illnesses have changed during the course of time. Inflammations have decreased, while the destructive illnesses have increased. Now we must concentrate on the question, if the spontaneous healing offered to us in the blessing of the fever is no longer present, if we ourselves must heal the predisposition, how will we manage it? In order to understand this better, let us compare someone who develops a malignant tumor with someone who develops an inflammation.

We know only too well what it means if someone lacks a healthy pink color, if he is pale and presents a sorrowful impression, especially if he is an elderly person. In the case of a malignant tumor, often the first thing to be observed is this pallor. There is no warmth, no perspiration, no increased activity of heartbeat and respiration.

We can now understand even better the value of a discovery made by Warburg, a German professor. At the beginning of this century, he discovered the difference between normal tissue respiration and tissue respiration around a tumor. Our lung respiration, the inhaling of oxygen and exhaling of carbon dioxide, permeates the depths of our body, reaching all tissues. The nutritious substances we receive are burnt up by the oxygen we inhale through the lungs. This results in water and carbon dioxide. In the aforementioned case of cancer, this "combustion" is *incomplete*, the result being lactic acid instead of water and carbon dioxide. Warburg called this "a suffocation of the tissues," an expression still used and accepted today. We clearly see that, instead of an intensification, we find an inhibition of respiration.

A third difference between inflammatory illnesses and cancer shows itself, for instance, in the consistency of an inflammatory tumor as opposed to a cancerous tumor. We may express this as the difference between something weak and something hard. Though an inflammatory tumor may be rigid in the beginning, it tends to soften, even to liquify. Again, we must understand that this is only the extreme example of the difference between inflammation and cancer, one in which the polarity shows itself in the clearest way.

When we contemplate typical examples of patients suffering from feverish illnesses—especially children who tend to run high fevers—and we compare this with the impression of a pale, emaciated person, whose appearance may fill us with anxiety, we can find yet another expression that joins the polarity of weakness and hardness. Someone with a high fever often gives the impression of being "in a cloud." It is as if the outline of his body is less clear, we could almost say "cosmic." Patients of the opposite type, with their neat, exact features, may then be called more "earthly." Weakness and hardness, now expressed as the cosmic and earthly, become still more comprehensible expressions when we relate the "cosmic" with warmth and respiration and the "earthly" with coolness and suffocation.

Inflammation belongs to youth as the tumor does to the later years. We could go even further and call inflammation principally Oriental, the tumor Occidental. I know quite well that today we cannot easily agree on this difference, but in 1920 we were taught that in the Orient cancer hardly ever occurred. It seems as if the conditions of the West have gradually expanded over the earth! In connection with the change of the image of illnesses in the course of evolution, we have already found that inflammation belongs to ancient times and the tumor to our own epoch. With these insights, we may draw the following diagram:

	Inflammation	Tumor	
	red	pale	
cosmic (in	warm	cool	earthly
a cloud)			(exact
less	perspiring	dry	features)
individual			far more
tendency	increased	"metabolic	individual
toward	respiration	suffocation"	tendency
restoration			toward
	young	aged	destruction
	more Oriental	more Occidental	
	ancient times	modern times	

One could say, of course, that we find inflammations also at the end of our life and that tumors may appear in our youth; we find cancer in the East and inflammations in the West; we might find examples of cancer in ancient times, while we still have inflammations in our times. The point is, however, that we are looking for the essential differences, for the polarity.

The most important difference remains the restoring tendency of inflammations and the destroying force of cancer. What happens? We see that in the case of an inflammation all the constructive forces of our body together enhance their activity and rush, so to speak, to the place of the disaster. In the case of cancer, we have to do with exactly the opposite: the formative forces retreat from a certain location, thus allowing the tumor to appear.

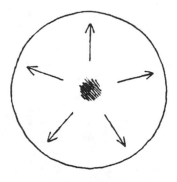   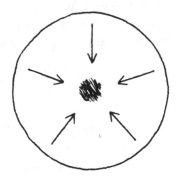

Inflammation appears   Cancer appears

The arrows indicate the
opposite directions of
the constructive forces
of our body.

What is a tumor? It is a growth. For years and years scientists have searched for the reason that cells in our body suddenly begin multiplying. The most sophisticated theories have been invented to explain this phenomenon. If we introduce the idea of the formative forces in our conception of the body, matters suddenly become clear. We should not ask first why a cell begins to grow but why generally it does *not* begin to grow; what forces keep it in its place? It is easy to recognize the activity of the formative forces that maintain our form, that is, our ego-organization. Now we can also understand that cancer originates in a retreat of those forces.

For the moment it is of no importance to consider the question of why cancer can begin to develop in so many places in our body; there are many more questions to be answered. The problem is very complicated, but the main principle is simple: the retreat of the constructive forces. This tendency to draw back or retreat is one of the aspects of the predisposition that results in the possibility of the tumor developing. If someone develops a cancer, it is not the beginning of the illness but the end, the final phase. The Swiss cancerologist, Dr. Werner Kaelin, called the tumor the last phase of a long tragedy; cancer he called a catastrophe of the form.

We have said already that cancer is defined as an illness that does not respect the anatomical structure. The anatomical structure is our living form in the most evident sense of the word: it is the result of the activity of the life-forces. The contrast between inflammation and cancer clearly shows what lies behind both illnesses. We can now also understand that the activity taking place in the feverish body depends on an activity of the constructive, the formative forces. Having met this idea first in the temple healing in Egypt, we can develop a deeper and deeper understanding of the mystery revealing itself in the restoring effect of the inflammation.

If, on the other hand, we have to do with a tumor,

with cancer, and think of the fact that the constructive
forces responsible for the anatomical structure retreat,
the tumor following that retreat, we begin to understand
better Dr. Kaelin's description of cancer as a catastrophe
of the form. We come also to the conclusion that removing the tumor is, essentially, never a real healing. It
makes no sense to speak of cases in which removing the
tumor was effective to the extent that it did not return,
that there was no recidivism. That may well be true, but
then we have to ask, what made the formative forces
"reverse their direction"? This, in fact, is the answer to
the question of whether something can be done to change
the condition in the living body so that, instead of a
retreat of the life-forces, we can produce again some activity able to maintain the form.

We also can understand the different phases of
cancer. The receding of the formative forces is not something that happens at once or in a regular, continuous
fashion. The course of cancer mainly shows a development in phases. First the local tumor develops, then the
enlargement of the regional lymphatic glands,* and finally dissemination throughout the body. It is well known
how varied the course of cancer can be. Often, a certain
phase can remain for years until the second one appears.
The primary tumor can develop enormously, and yet the
regional glands may be relatively little enlarged. In other
cases, the primary tumor can be very small while, in a
short time, the region of the lymph glands begins to
develop. There are even cases in which the primary
tumor hardly develops at all, whereas in a short time the
whole body is permeated by metastases. Here, science has

---

*The secondary tumors, following the primary tumors in the next phase, are
called metastases.

introduced the word "malignity," cancer being called a malignant tumor. We need not do away with this expression, but it should be understood that the malignity is not situated so much in the tumor itself but rather in the lack of resistance toward its growth, in the giving in of the formative forces and the speed with which these forces retreat.

Comparison of inflammation and cancer gives us the possibility of surveying the whole of our historical consideration and finding its connection with our own daily experiences. What restored the body in the Egyptian era? We spoke about creating, shaping forces and related them to spiritual beings. In the case of fever, we find creating forces in the body whose activity is enhanced, and the result is restoration. In my view, it is as if the same thing that later manifested itself in fever took place in Egypt, though in a less physical way. We could even speak of a healing bath both in the case of fever and of temple healings, of being submerged in the realm of the restoring formative forces.

Coming to the beginning of our era, we mentioned the great epidemics. They were first of all feverish illnesses; hundreds and thousands of people suddenly were stricken with high fevers, certainly many hundreds of thousands—or more—died, though many also survived. I think we should not make the mistake that has been mentioned so often already and say that those epidemics have always been and are still happening. The nature of illness has changed fundamentally since then as, in the course of a long time, in thousands of years, humanity has also changed in every respect, mentally as well as physically. The great epidemics existed in a time in which man had a special constitution, different from the times before and different from present times. These great epidemics have gradually disappeared. I am not forgetting, of course, the great flu epidemic of 1918, but I must, at the same time, call to mind the very special mental situation in which humanity lived at that time in modern Europe. I am also not forgetting that we continually have flu epidemics, but we should look for the differences between these and the epidemics we have called the "scourge of God."

1918 is more than half a century ago. How much humanity has changed even since then! We have spoken about evolution holding its breath in the nineteenth century. It is as if, in our century, we are confronted with exactly the opposite phenomenon. There is a running, a rushing toward the future, leaving the past far behind. However, toward the future means, in our case, toward earth, toward an incredible increase in specialization and individualization. In connection with this, I would like to recall something that tends to be forgotten, which is interesting enough in itself! In 1920 we were given a lecture on the symptoms of pneumonia. The clinical picture was very exact and minute: someone, say at 4:20 p.m., suddenly feels a sharp pain in his back; he has contracted a chill, begins to cough, and expectorates *"sputa rufa,"* brownish sputum. Blisters (herpes) develop on his lips. A high fever sets in with regular undulations: *"febris continua."* The patient feels very ill, and in the course of days, especially on the fifth and on the sixth days, the symptoms, fever and misery, come to a climax. On the seventh day (in rare cases on the ninth day), suddenly, the fever disappears. At the same time, the patient feels quite well again, feels even reborn. This fall of temperature was called the crisis, and the increase in symptoms just before the crisis was called the ante-critical aggravation: *"perturbatio ante-critica."*

I have given the pathography in this way to show how we became acquainted with the typical images of special illnesses. At the same time we were taught that the more typical the symptoms were, the better the prognosis was. At the end of my medical studies we were informed, however, that the typical pictures of illnesses were disappearing. A pneumonia did not necessarily develop suddenly anymore, neither did the diseased condition necessarily end abruptly any longer. We could imagine that the forces of restoration, the forces of recovering, were showing a tendency to decline. We may conclude that humanity was apparently losing its capacity for producing fever! I know this is a daring supposition, but to me it makes sense.

In which period of life do we still encounter epidemic-like, feverish illnesses? In childhood, in youth. Children are still capable of producing fever, just as it is not difficult to understand that children still show in their constitution qualities of a phase through which the whole of humanity passed in its evolution.

Let us recapitulate the whole picture: in the Egyptian era, creating, restoring forces could penetrate the human bodies directly during the temple sleep. It was an age of group-people. In the course of time, the same restoring activity could be effected only in the form of (high) fevers with deeply penetrating influences of the same forces. In the following centuries, man's constitution began to change; the possibility of such penetration was gradually limited to the period of childhood as, at the same time, man became more individualized or "emancipated." In contrast to this development, the other illnesses, which show less restoring activity, have increased parallel to man's becoming more and more "earthly."

We have said already that it makes no sense to mention the fact that fever does occur at all ages. It does occur, of course, but we can get the right impression, as I have tried to outline, only when we look at the whole picture from a distance, when we survey the total from as far away as possible. I said in the section called "Introduction" that science, certainly medical science, makes the mistake of looking at the phenomena from too close. What we must learn to do is to look not through magnifying but through "minifying" glasses.

The two types of illness, inflammation and cancer, enframe, so to speak, the totality of all remaining illnesses. These cannot be considered "*in extenso*"; the main characteristic is that they have one principal thing in common: they stick more or less to an organ or system, the rest of the body being much less involved, if at all. We could perhaps express this by saying that it is never the whole body that is concerned.

In cancer we came upon an illness with a different aspect. We speak of breast cancer, stomach cancer, uterine cancer, etc., but in reality there is only cancer with a different beginning point. Even the fact that different cancers may have different prognoses does not diminish the fact that cancer does not stick to a single organ or system. The expression, "Cancer does not respect anatomical boundaries," speaks for itself. So far, we have seen that inflammation and cancer are real opposites.

The remaining illnesses show some peculiarities important for our investigations. These have already been summed up roughly (see pages 81-82) as illnesses of the bones, of muscles and the nervous system, of the heart and vessels, of blood, and of organs. We have to do with illnesses for which the term "degenerative processes" is often used. Yet nearly always we find inflammatory symptoms accompanying the further development, either at the beginning or continually.

It is as if we still experience the favorable influence of some restoring activity, which allows these illnesses, as much as possible, to stick to their organ or system. It is also understandable that in the course of history these illnesses must have increased in number and have become more—we could best describe it—"expressed." We should also expect them to appear later in life. Is this not correct? Do not the illnesses of the bones and muscles (rheumatic illnesses), of the central and peripheral nervous system, of the heart and vessels, of the metabolism and the organs, belong to a later period in human life, later than youth with its epidemic childhood illnesses? Have not these illnesses increased in the world in such a way that the increase in cancer is the end of the story? And have not all the illnesses I've mentioned, cancer included, the common tendency to be progressive? Everyone can make his own reply, should judge by himself.

Rheumatism, however, can be found in youth also, in the acute rheumatoid arthritis of young children. It is an illness beginning with high fever and clear inflammatory symptoms in the joints, which do, however, tend to heal. Though there can be long aftereffects, this does not weaken the pattern. An acute illness of the nervous-sense system also occurs in youth: infantile paralysis. Here too we observe fever and inflammation. In spite of the fact that there may be terrible aftereffects—even invalidism— it is well known that the process always tends to come to a definite standstill. On the other hand, we know about an inflammatory illness with high fever that is found in adolescence and that shows little tendency of healing: it is an inflammation of the valves of the heart (endocarditis lenta), which mainly ended in death in earlier times.*

Cancer has been characterized as a disease that does

---

*This is one of the diseases in which antibiotic treatment has experienced one of its greatest successes.

not respect the anatomical boundaries. In spite of the fact that we know of ever-so-many differences in prognoses and malignities, we *do* speak of cancer in general. The maintaining forces show no limit in their retreat. "Maintaining forces" are those forces that maintain our bodies from birth to death. Death means the moment these forces give up their activity of maintenance. Cancer, thus far, anticipates the character of death during life. I think this is one of the reasons that there is so much fear regarding cancer.

One group of illnesses we have left untouched, the so-called psychiatric illnesses. Psychiatric patients are bearers of deformations that do not show themselves so concretely as the "general" illness does. Of course, there are definite deformations as well, but they must be considered as anomalies of the life-body, showing their physical side primarily, although slightly, in the realm of metabolism. The feeling that the prognosis for these illnesses is not, on the whole, favorable is partly due to the fact that the possibility of eliminating a deforming trouble through a physical illness is reduced to a minimum. We could say, "The cloud does not give rain." Considering why this is the case would lead us beyond the limits of this book.

Illness and the Human Constitution

In speaking of predisposition, we have, from the beginning, used the word "deformation," a deformation of the life-body. This deformation is the principal origin of an illness. Can we have any idea what this concept of deformation expresses? Can we have any idea what a deformation of the life-body means? A deformation in the physical body is not difficult to imagine, because we know the body's structure to a large extent. The organization of the life-body, however, is not static; it is a body of forces. Studying the total form of a physical body is one way of getting a slight idea of it. We have to pass over from an exact picture into the realm of those forces from which that picture has been created. This requires an artistic approach. Speaking of a "composition" has implied this same attitude from the beginning.

The polarity between inflammation and cancer stands in close connection with another polarity that we find in the human body. To understand this, we must study the human shape in a new way, as the result of the ego-organization. One of the fundamental conceptions about the human being that will help us in this direction is that of the threefold composition of the human body. It was Rudolf Steiner who developed this threefold picture in the years before 1917 when he, for the first time, spoke about it in his book, *Riddles of the Soul*. He distinguished between three systems: the nerve-sense system, the rhythmic system, and the metabolic-limb system. These systems, in short, head, chest, and trunk, are not exact anatomical parts but functional parts of our body. Each element permeates our whole body, though having its main activity in its own area. We could even circumscribe these areas of activity by saying, at the top, *head*; in the middle, *chest*; at the bottom, *trunk*.

The rhythmic system, the chest, shows its qualities not only in the rhythmic movements of respiration and heartbeat but in the physical image of the repetition of forms in the vertebral column and in the ribs of the chest. The threefold composition of man reveals a certain law shown in the polarity of the head and the trunk, with the chest as a transition in the center.

Considering the head, we see that it is round, quiet, and cool. At the other pole, the metabolic-limb system, we find the opposite qualities: radiation, mobility, warmth. The qualities of roundness and quiet in relation to the head will be accepted by most people. Coolness is expressed not only in comments such as "keep a cool head" but also in the wish for a cool cloth on the forehead when we have a headache. The metabolic-limb system is the pole of warmth; we want a hot-water bottle when we have abdominal pain. In the case of the mediating rhythmic system, we will have to elaborate a little. If we take the head, for a moment, as the pole of rest and the lower part of the body as the pole of movement, we can apply a fundamental law to the rhythmic system. Wherever a tendency toward rest meets a tendency toward movement, a rhythm appears at the place of the meeting. The bow of a violin, moving over strings, causes rhythmic swinging. The meeting of sea, wind, and sand on the beach leaves behind the ripple of ridges we all know so well. Are we not reminded of the ribs and vertebrae?

Now, we can perform an amusing and instructive experiment. If one holds a burning cigarette without moving and looks at the rising pillar of smoke (the air must be totally quiet, people must be silent), we perceive a moving current meeting quiet air. A cloud of smoke is formed, but, at the transition of the smoke pillar into the cloud, we will see a short but wonderfully clear rhythmic dancing, three or four times. I can only advise the reader to try to enjoy this phenomenon.

The polarity between the nerve-sense system and the metabolic-limb system shows yet another element not mentioned previously. In our brain, the central part of our nerve-sense system, we have to do with nerve cells, which lack the capacity to reproduce. If, on the other hand, we think of the vitality of a white blood corpuscle, a leukocyte, as well as of other cells of our metabolic system, we find just the opposite. Indeed, when our brain cells are shut off from the blood circulation, if only for a few seconds, they cannot remain alive. This is what occurs in a stroke. We can see that our nerve-sense system bears the stamp of death. Nobody should be surprised or frightened by this fact; we should understand that our brain is the instrument with which man is able to think *just because* of the fact that our brain has hardly any life of its own. Here we will have to face many prejudices that have been created in the course of the centuries. The sentence, "We think with our brains," as has already been explained, does not mean that our brain thinks. On the contrary, the moment we fall asleep, the brain becomes more alive than when we are awake, which is also shown in the so-called electroencephalogram. We should not forget that in our perceiving and thinking life, which is in reality our life in the world of the senses and the life of our thoughts, we have to do with life which is, so to speak, sacrificed by our brain. Consciousness and bodily life are opposites in which the life of the body is sacrificed to that of the consciousness.

We find a wonderful illustration of this when we look on life as a whole. In the beginning, a child lives very much in his body. His consciousness is just beginning to come into being. When we think of an old person, we can often feel that he is living in a strong world of consciousness, paralleling the fact that he is losing physical vitality. The center of consciousness, however, is, from the beginning, in the head. Look at a child's head, how much more alive it appears. It is as if death-forces gradually take possession of our body from head to foot; in other words, head forces are penetrating our body more and more in the course of life.

If we look at the other side of the body, the limbs, we

have the pole of our physical activity, the pole of our actions. It is wonderful to study the contrast between mental and physical activity. We can easily see how actively children live in their limbs. The metabolic-limb system is clearly the life pole with its vitality, warmth, and physical mobility.

When we look at the human shape in this way, speaking about the polarity between life and death, warmth and coolness, mobility and rest, youth and age, we come to understand that man lives as a healthy being only when he finds a rhythmic balance between these polarities. In our respiration, in our heartbeat, we are continually moving between these opposites. Our heart moves between systole and diastole, our breath between inspiration and expiration, our life between attention and relaxation, between thinking activity and life activity. Attention is only possible when it alternates with inattention, albeit in a very subtle way. We can go on to see that even day and night, consciousness and sleep, are further examples of the rhythmic life of man.

Let us put it this way: the healthy life of man is possible only if it unfolds itself in a harmonious equilibrium between life and death. This very sentence expresses our method of investigation. We are not studying the totality by looking at the details, but instead we are coming to understand the details by studying the whole.

Think of Paracelsus. He, too, described man (and the plant) as a threefold being, speaking of salt (sal), mercury, and sulfur. If we try to characterize the three principles by looking at their representatives in the mineral world, it is not difficult to see the relationships. Sulfur: the warm, "burning pole"; salt: the quiet, cool pole; mercury (think of the peculiar quality of mercury, of spreading out into little drops and coming together again): expansion and contraction, a rhythmic process. In short, we have polarities, united by a rhythmic principle.

Illness is always in some way accompanied by the predominance of one of the polarities. So far, we have recognized the two opposites, warmth and coolness. There is, at the same time, another way of characterizing this polarity, as chaos and order. Chaos, the realm of the metabolic system (the realm of movement) is the opposite of the realm of order, form, regularity, etc. Our symmetrical form clearly has its origin in the head, the brain. This symmetry extends, of course, into the very depths of our body. The chaos of metabolism, on the other hand, keeps our whole body alive by forces that work in an upward direction.

A wonderful illustration of this polarity can be found in the activity of our intestines, a convolution of warm, living, hollow, ever-changing windings. The brain, where we also speak of windings, shows a typical similarity and contrast at the same time. The brain has a wonderfully symmetrical form, whereas the intestines are asymmetrical. In the brain we have cool, death-like, solid, quiet forms. This similarity is not the result of an abstract study and a conclusion of wishful thinking; it is the result of an experience with pupils at a high school where, as I was drawing a picture of the brain on the blackboard, one of the boys asked, "Are you going to lecture us about the intestines?" One has the feeling that in the brain we are shown the *result* of our activity, which has to a great extent left behind the form, while in our intestines we see the activity still at work. As we have called this activity "life," we might conclude that in our intestines life is fully engaged in the processes that take place in the field of digestion. In the brain that same life has been, for the most part, "squeezed out" of the physical organ, appearing in our consciousness as the life of our thoughts and our perceptions.

With illness, with conditions in which the balance between the two poles is lost, we see that the "tendency of life" may prevail, developing a condition of chaos throughout the body, giving man a cloud-like appearance, as we have seen in the case of fever. The tendency of death may intensify to such an extent that the body seems to fall apart when the life-forces are no longer capable of maintaining their form. That is the case with inflammation, and now we must deal with cancer.

Cancer and Psychosomatism

Cancer is an illness of our time; we should not doubt for a moment that cancer has clearly increased in the last hundred years; so have quite a number of destructive illnesses. Comparing the present situation with the ancient Egyptian era, we can hardly imagine a greater contrast, not forgetting that in the time following the Egyptian epoch, in the Greek period, we have the onset of our modern-day thinking, which begins with philosophy; we have seen great transitions in the area of human consciousness. These few remarks are meant to introduce the problem of the increase of cancer in our century, an important fact we cannot deny.

Bring to mind once more what I was told at the university in 1920 when I was a student, that cancer did not exist in the Orient. We could say that where Western civilization and technology advanced, cancer clearly followed. We can understand this phenomenon if we remind ourselves of the supposition that all illnesses have their beginning points in the psyche. We have already seen that this can be valid only if we begin to accept the idea of reincarnation, at least as a possibility. Only then does such a conclusion about general psychosomatism become relevant.

What does it mean to say, "Where Western civilization appears, cancer follows"? It means that we must find a link between our civilization and the life of our soul, which should somehow throw a light on the physical symptoms of cancer. How can we characterize the change in the soul life brought about by Occidental influences? How do we characterize life in the West? Are we not confronted with rush hours and traffic jams, appointment books filled with engagements, no time to spare, no breathing space? Life suffocates us. Do we not find a decrease of interest in the life of our fellow men? Is not egotism increasing from day to day? Is there not an increasing lack of enthusiasm for life? Love, enthusiasm warmth of the heart, all are in danger. Cynicism, a lack of respect for man's existence, the ridicule of religion, a decline in art, and so on, come to the foreground instead. The word cynicism is derived from the Greek word "*kyoon*," which means dog. A dog sniffs with his nose over the ground, and thus cynicism implies earthliness. It is clear that materialism has played an important role in bringing about this cynical attitude. Suffocated, cool, earthly, all are the expressions that we have met in discussing the nature of cancer. In this way modern times create a predisposition for cancer. The psychic influence of our environment, as we have mentioned, is responsible for turning a predisposition into an illness. The chemical, physical, biological factors and also the psychic influences, can cause an illness, however, only if there is a predisposition.

It is clear that not everyone is equally vulnerable to the aforementioned influences. We could explain this

problem in the following way: the psychosomatic influences belong to a category of general influences that apply more or less to everyone in a certain time period. The
predisposition, on the other hand, is that very individual
side of the problem that shows us why only certain people
are affected by influences from without. We thus understand that the word predisposition contains many more
elements than we have considered up to this point.

So often the question is asked why so many people to
whom the words "suffocated," "cool," and "earthly," do
not apply still get cancer. So many artists get it too. My
answer is that we should not wonder at this. If we think
of someone who is an exponent of his time, who is born
and bred in and adapted to Western civilization, it is not
surprising that such a person is able to meet the problems
of our time in a better way than the artists, who in their
inner constitutions are perhaps far less adapted to it. We
should never forget that no one is able to remove himself
entirely from the influences of his time. Whoever he is,
whenever he lives, and whatever he does, he sees the
things that are made, he hears the sounds that are produced, he reads the books that are written, and he thinks
the thoughts that are thought. It is not too far-fetched to
think that we may find cancer cases there where we
would not have expected them.

These examples of the qualities of modern civilization
can, of course, by no means explain the origin of cancer.
They should be considered as a description of circumstances which, combined with the change in the consistency of the human body, enhance the possibility of developing cancer. The predisposition itself, which time and
again contains the answer to the question why, under the
same circumstances, one person falls ill and another does
not, shows itself from the beginning in the psychic consti-

tution of the individual. Here we may content ourselves
with the rather well-known evidence that what is sometimes called the "cancer psyche" shows itself, among other
ways, in an introverted character. Indeed, the opposite
can also be understood. Extroversion obviously belongs to
youth and to the opposite kind of illness: inflammation.*

In the next chapter we will try to discover the possibilities for a new understanding of healing. We will con-
fine ourselves to the problem of cancer, as it offers us a
clear example. To me, it remains of great importance not
to forget that the tumor itself is not the illness but rather
merely a symptom. We have even seen that the tumor
tends to do away with the predisposition. Our task will be
to discover how we can heal the predisposition so that the
illness does not have to do it. This means that we must
change our attitude toward the tumor: instead of fighting
it, we must try to take over its task. On the other hand,
we will also have to occupy ourselves with the psychic
side of the problem. Trying to do away with the physical
part of the illness would be only half the work.

Everything said until now must be taken into account. As we have seen, humanity gradually forgot about
healing after the time of Hippocrates, as his relationship
to the kingdoms of nature changed from early times up to
the present. The first thing we must do is to ask: how can
we create such a relationship anew, not forgetting that
this new relationship will have to be established in accordance with our modern consciousness?

---

*Recently, when speaking about the increase in cancer in our day, someone
gave me information about an old, experienced practitioner. He had said,
"Cancer is the laughing that has not been laughed, is the weeping that has not
been wept." I think this is an interesting saying, which on another level implies
the problem of "suffocation" or lack of respiration.

The Practice of Healing: The Evolution
in the Kingdoms of Nature

To become more familiar with the reality of the predisposition so as to find a way to overcome it, it is
necessary, for the moment, to penetrate deeply into a
totally different realm of anthropology, the realm of
human evolution. Humanity in general seems to have accepted the theory that the human being has evolved out
of the animal. The sequence of animals, as they are
thought to have appeared on the earth, gives a picture of
what has happened from the distant past up to the present: the so-called higher animals have evolved out of the
lower ones. Man was the last stage, appearing after the
apes. Evolutionists study how this evolution took place.
Lamarck, Darwin, the mutationists, Haeckel, and others
have all contributed to the establishment of evolutionary
theory. The main principles of evolution of the animal
form are adaptation to the environment, natural selection, survival of the fittest, and mutations.

Has science succeeded in giving a general accepted explanation? Definitely not. In spite of all its efforts, two
hundred years have not sufficed to satisfy the need for a
real, accepted, comprehensible solution to the problem of
man's evolution.

One problem is that, as a consequence of the thought
that man evolved out of the animals, we have to imagine
that the kingdom of the animals emerged out of the kingdom of the plants. This, in turn, must have been the result
of events that happened in the world of the minerals.

| mineral kingdom | plant kingdom | animal kingdom | man |

How the mineral world came into being will, of course, always remain a riddle. The problem is generally solved by saying that "in the beginning there was a primeval explosion." That is not much of an explanation, though.

We cannot cover all the arguments on evolution here. I must limit myself to giving a succinct summary of the contents of evolution in the light of spiritual science, as described in Rudolf Steiner's book, *An Outline of Occult Science.** More than ever it will be necessary to avoid prejudices; for the moment, let us consider only whether or not this information provides an answer to our questions. In these revelations, we are dealing not with hypotheses but with perceptions through organs of sense of a different nature from the sense organs we use in daily life.** The following is meant to give a clear picture of the evolution of the earth—or, what is the same thing, the evolution of the kingdoms of nature and humanity.

---

*Rudolf Steiner, *An Outline of Occult Science,* Anthroposophic Press, Spring Valley, N.Y., 1979, in the chapter, "World Development and Man."

**The results of the study of the spiritual world, which might also be called the world of the creating beings, have been described in several works by Rudolf Steiner. The obvious question is what to do with communications that we cannot verify, at least not for the time being. Rudolf Steiner answers this question clearly in his book, *Knowledge of the Higher Worlds and its Attainment* Anthroposophic Press, Spring Valley, N.Y., 1983:

> "In order to establish the facts through research, the ability to enter the supersensible worlds is indispensable; but once they have been discovered and communicated, even one who does not perceive them himself can be adequately convinced of their truth. A large proportion of them can be tested offhand, simply by applying ordinary common sense in a genuinely unprejudiced way. Only, one must not let this open-mindedness become confused by any of the preconceived ideas so common in human life. Someone can easily believe, for example, that some statement or other contradicts certain facts established by modern science. In reality, there is no such thing as a scientific fact that contradicts spiritual science."

In the beginning, creating beings, whom we have also called gods or hierarchies—the name is for the moment of no importance—created man as a physical being out of the substance "warmth." In a second phase, life was added to the "physical" warmth-body, life being given by another group of hierarchical beings. The "physical" substance in part became more dense, and a gaseous condition was the result. An "air" phase thus was reached. In the third phase, man was endowed with a consciousness; a soul life

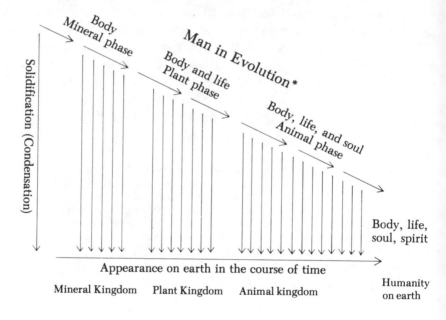

*It should be emphasized that the events that took place as described in *Occult Science* are far more intricate and complicated. The above is only a simple diagram to indicate the essential ideas.

was created in him, while the substance turned partly into liquid—a "water" phase thus came into existence. In the fourth and final phase, man was given a spirit-element, his ego, and the physical substance was solidified to "earth."

It is important to understand that in each phase one part did not continue to develop but remained behind. What remained behind from the first phase evolved, after an unimaginably long time, into our mineral kingdom or purely physical matter. What remained behind in the second phase became our kingdom of the plants. A plant is composed of a physical body and of life. Out of the third phase our kingdom of the animals arose; there we have physical body, life, and soul. The last to appear was the human being, having a physical body, life, soul, and spirit.

From this description, it becomes clear that man himself was never an animal or a plant or a mineral but went through the phases of these three kingdoms. The kingdoms themselves, which we now have around us, are the part of our evolution that has remained behind, separated from man.

To discuss the riddle of human evolution at length goes beyond the context of this book, but it might be sensible, in order to feel something of the essence of the picture of the evolution of humanity, to ask oneself: does it make a difference to me whether I consider the human being as the result of a long creative process, standing between a past and a future, or whether I must look at that same being merely as a product of chance? I think it is a general truth that we all are looking for solutions that satisfy our entire beings, not only our heads but also our

hearts.* We should remind ourselves that the conception
of man as an evolved animal, giving up the idea of a creating God, was strongly opposed. It took nearly half a
century before man became accustomed to such new
thoughts. In the same way, we should not wonder that
the introduction of new conceptions (which is not going
back to early believing) meets with the same resistance.

The Kingdom of the Animals and Human Evolution

For our purpose we must consider more closely the
transition of the plant phase of humanity into the animal
phase. First of all we must ask, what is the essence of a

---

*To elaborate in a satisfying way on this problem of evolution by comparing the
two views that have been mentioned would, as has been said, lead too far
afield. I should like only to give a little hint of a link between the two conceptions. This comes from something experienced by the previously mentioned anthropologist, Bolk. Bolk came into possession of a six month old chimpanzee.
He was struck by the fact that this little being was naked, had hair only on its
head, had a forehead and a chin. In short, it looked very much like a human
baby.

According to Haeckel's fundamental law of biogenetics, the higher animal
goes through the phases of the lower ones in his development from egg cell to
final form. Thinking of man as an evolved ape, he might expect that man
should pass through an ape-like phase before birth. Here he experienced the
opposite, however. He saw an ape showing a human aspect before birth. His
only conclusion could be that the ape stems from man in some way. Geniuses
can discover fundamental laws out of relatively few phenomena (just as
Haeckel had done); Bolk's conclusion was that such a phenomenon could make
sense only if he was allowed to suppose that the whole kingdom of animals had
emerged out of humanity's evolution.

The diagram we have given on page 154 shows that principle in a clear way.
Bolk himself added, "The result of my supposition is that man is no longer a
random result of evolution; this thought highly satisfies me."

Of course, this little addition certainly cannot really fill the gap between the
two conceptions of evolution. I think it is important to show, however, that
the revelations of spiritual science may easily link with suppositions in the
realm of earthly science, if these are based on clear phenomena.

plant? A plant is an "open" being, fully connected with its environment, in its roots, leaves, and flowers as well; it is a being consisting of lines and surfaces. In the life of the plants, the seasons of the year are revealed; I could define the plant as follows: the plant is an open image of life between earth and heaven (the cosmos).

An animal is quite different. An animal has an inward life; awareness and motion are its main qualities. From them we may conclude that the animal has a soul life. The reason that evolutionists have not succeeded in explaining animal evolution is that they have looked at the animal as a living *form*. Certainly, the animal *has* a living form, but it *is* something else: the animal is, above all, a desire! What does this mean? Let us put it this way: in each species of animal lives a particular form of desire, a specific one. The word specific means that the idea of desire should not be separated from the word instinct, or instinct connected desire, which enables us to give a more clear description of the specific desire in each species of animals. Which desire lives in each particular animal, in a snail, in a snake, in a lion? The desire to be a snail, a snake, a lion! Hence the conclusion that an animal is a visible desire.* We can understand this by realizing that a desire always asks for satisfaction, knows, so to speak, about nothing else. An animal must live, therefore, in an environment providing it with the possibility of satisfying its needs. Hence the strong relationship between animal and environment. At the same time we receive the possibility of understanding the unity of the phenomena: animal desire, animal shape, and animal environment!

---

*We may remind ourselves of similar statements in which we have said: an animal has no predisposition, it *is* a predisposition; an animal has no talent, it *is* a talent.

We may define the animal as a oneness of desire, shape, and environment. This leads to the conclusion that an animal can never evolve. An animal can improve, but only a being that *has* desires can evolve.

The sequence of the animal groups, from the one-celled animals to the mammals, shows a wonderful image of evolution. In the beginning we see open, plant-related animals, for which water, air, and warmth still form the environment. Water, as circulation, air, as respiration (beginning in the amphibians), and warmth (beginning as its own warmth-organization in birds and mammals), turn inward, gradually moving inside the animal. The increase in inward life is obvious. This inward life, however, is a life of desire. We will try to understand what it means that this kingdom was separated from humanity in the course of his evolution.

Humanity evolved out of the plant phase into the animal phase. We have already considered the plant as something entirely open to its environment, its roots to the soil, its leaves to the air, and its flowers to the sunlight, which also belongs to the physical world! The animal, as we have seen, is a being with an inner life. Man changed from a being fully connected with his environment into one separated from it, chiefly by the organs of sense, this separation being a condition for awareness. There is a fundamental law that says, to be connected with something and to perceive something are two conditions that mutually exclude one another. Perception, or awareness, demands separation!

As man began to separate from his environment, he began as a result to perceive that same environment. What was the environment? The creative world, creative beings. This is why in mythology, which speaks of this important transition, we always hear about creating be-

ings, about gods! We have already gone into this subject
in the section, "Knowing and Believing." We may now go
one step further and ask what has happened to change
man's consciousness so intensely. It is what is described in
the Bible as the "fall of man." Again, the reader should
not think that I am taking the Bible authoritatively, but I
may take the Biblical facts and make use of them as long
as I do nothing more than consider them as phenomena.
In the Bible we hear about Lucifer (the serpent), a spiritual being, approaching humanity and adding desire to
his perceptions. We have seen how this included a change
of awareness, of consciousness; out of this change, the
world of our senses gradually developed.

We must bear in mind at this moment that the bodily
consistency of man and world in that epoch was not yet as
solid as it is now. Because of this, the seduction of Lucifer
created a great danger, which can best be explained in
the following example. If we imagine a group of chil
dren, window shopping, looking at sweets (or toys), we
hear, "Oh, look at that wonderful . . .; Oh no, look here,
isn't this exciting . . .," etc. The children's eyes pop out
of their heads; in Holland we have the expression, their
eyes are mounted on stalks. This is only a way of speaking. The children do not have eyes on stalks, of course! In
a former period, however, this danger was real: man
might have developed deformations such as eyes on
stalks. Of course, if we continue our thoughts in a logical
way, we may add: not only eyes but also "ears on stalks,"
"mouths on stalks," "noses on stalks." Man would have
developed a form which, in comparison to the appropriate one, would have been a deformation. The only
way to save man from such a deformation was to create a
kingdom that could embody the superfluity of desires, thus
allowing him to maintain the ability to develop his human

shape. The animal, thereby, would take on the human being's desires, would *be* the desire, which as we have said already is the correct description of the animal.*

Now we are able to give another definition of the animal: the animal is the embodiment of a deformation that otherwise would have inhibited human evolution. The reader will recognize that this is the same definition we gave to illness. To speak of such a relationship between illness and the animal may sound unbelievable, may even seem senseless, just a play on words. This impression may change, however, if, instead of speaking of a relationship, we use the expression, to recognize a relationship. Considering the creation of the animal kingdom as it has been described causes us to regard this creation at the same time as a healing process during the evolution of man, a *cosmic healing*. We can also come to see that illness can be considered as a healing process that still accompanies us after the fulfillment of the evolution of our human shape.

To appreciate the idea that the influence of the desires on the human form would indeed have caused an unfavorable deformation, we should return for a moment to the description of the threefold nature of the human being. We must try to understand that man, as a thinking, feeling, and willing being, is an unique phenomenon in the whole of nature. Man, upright, speaking, and thinking, himself a creating being, can bear witness to the

---

*An illustration of "the animal" in man, the fact that man is not free from desires, from "animals," is one of the reasons we find so many animal expressions, animal names, in curses, for example, to characterize others. We call our fellow men names like dog, pig, swine, rat, mouse, duck, goose, vulture, a snake in the grass, toad ("toady"); we use descriptions like slippery as an eel, industrious as a spider, busy as a bee, worm your way, to come out of your shell, and so on.

divine on earth. Perhaps we can look at his threefold nature as an image of the Trinity; perhaps we can look on man as a "creation after the image of God." Since this recognition creates the possibility of finding a new path for healing, this will be our next subject.

The Kingdom of the Plants and Human Evolution

To compare the animal and illness is certainly not usual. The definitions given, however, bring the two together and offer new, wide-ranging insight into the mystery of illness. This comparison, the animal and illness, will allow us to answer the question: how can we do away with the predisposition other than through illness itself? For this reason we must look at the plant kingdom in the same way as we investigated the animal world.

We might begin by asking what we owe to the plant. What do the plants give us, what do they signify? Firstly we may think of food, also perhaps of herbs. Other "blessings" of the plant kingdom are, most definitely, flowers, the fact that a spontaneous human soul would find it difficult to live without flowers! Flowers are given on so many occasions: birth, birthdays, engagements, weddings, illness, and finally death. Flowers accompany us through our life. Also consider that the plant kingdom provides us with oxygen, that it is the very source of our wood, coal, and oil supplies and therefore of our warmth; consider that the roots of the plants and the trees hold together the arable earth (without plants the earth would become a desert—think of the disastrous consequences of deforestation, for example). When we consider these things we begin to marvel at the "vital" significance of plant *life* on earth. As the animal is related to the soul, the plant is related to life.

From the summary regarding the evolution of man, we learn that we must accustom ourselves to the idea that man passed through not only an animal phase but also a plant phase. In the diagram of page 156 we indicated that the former phases took place in less densified conditions in the past. The plant phase of man must, of course, be imagined to have taken place under very different conditions from those today. Yet, without difficulty, we can still recognize in man the result of his development in his plant phase. We only have to look at the entire living human body.

The threefold nature of the body has already been described. It is not difficult to discover the same principle in the plant form. We have only to look critically at our observations. In the plant we generally distinguish roots, stalks, leaves, and flowers. When we draw a simple picture of a flowering plant, we can probably recognize the threefold composition of man. The roots are the quiet, cool, more-or-less rounded part; the flowers, the top of the plant, are the radiating counterpart where most of the changes take place during the year and where the plant opens itself toward its environment, to the light and warmth of the sun. Turning back to the roots of the plant, we can ask, how do we know a plant has roots? We know by pulling it out of the earth. The roots grow in the earth; they belong to the earth as the earth belongs to the roots. When we apply the same principle to the flower and realize how it is connected with the sun, with the cosmos (not poetically but physically, as light and warmth are physical!), we develop a totally new picture of the plant kingdom: seeing the earth as the center ("the head"), the plant lives as a being between center and periphery. Leaves and stalk are a picture of identical forms that are rhythmically repeated. We see a wonderful rhythm (not in time but in space) and a surprising link between earth (the quiet pole) and cosmos (the changing pole).

Looking at the forms of the organs in the human body along with their anatomical and histological construction, it is fascinating to observe the similarity of these forms to those in the kingdom of the plants. The most obvious example is found in the lungs. The "bronchial tree" (*bronchus* means branch) has a windpipe, large bronchies, small bronchies in their ramifications (*ramus* also means branch, a botanic word), and air-sacks. It is the image of an air-tree, surrounded by red substance, inhaling oxygen and exhaling carbon dioxide. The tree in nature, by contrast, is a substantial tree surrounded by air, is green, and inhales carbon dioxide and exhales oxygen.

We can find many more illustrations of relations between forms in man and plant. Each gland has, histolog-

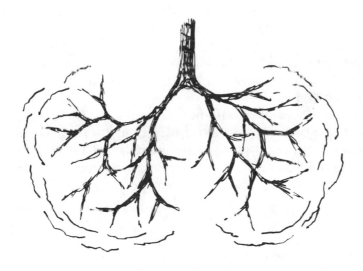

Drawing of the bronchial tree

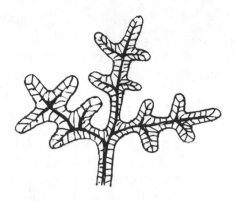

Drawing of glandular cells

ically speaking, a plant-related structure. The glandular cells, lying in neat lines along the ducts, show this unmistakably.

Not only is a certain analogy the main point but also the fact that several different analogies express the same principle. Even in special organs, such as our teeth, we find a crown and a root, expressions showing how strongly anatomists have recognized the plant structures in the human body.*

A last example should not be omitted. It is the picture of a plant, drawn in such a way that the rounded tendency in the root-pole of the plant is indicated on one side; on the other side radiating lines are drawn (of course in a very arbitrary way!) to indicate the connection be-

---

*Comparing animal with man, we heard about animal names being used for qualities in the soul of man. In the same way we come upon words by which we express qualities of the human body through plant names. We speak, for example, of cherry lips, rosebud mouth, peachy skin, apple cheeks, cauliflower ears, bulbous nose, a budding girl, and so on.

tween the flower and the environment, working from without. *In turning the drawing upside-down, the impression of a human shape is clearly recognized.*

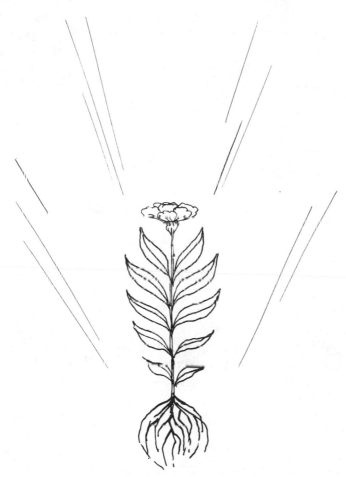

Drawing of a plant's structure

We cannot ask the question, what did the human form look like at the beginning of evolution? Hardly any form had materialized! It is impossible to think that the conditions in those times allow us to depict an image of the human being that is comparable to our present body. The human form must have been far more "extended," if we are to use an expression of space at all. Yet, dealing with all facts and data mentioned so far will by and by create the possibility of finding a way into events in evolution in the past when circumstances were so very different. Yet, what is the origin of the aforementioned similarity? We must return to our previous diagram of evolution. Before man entered into the animal phase, he went through the plant phase. His body then showed even less similarity to his present appearance.

In so far as the animal kingdom separated, as excessive desires were taken away from humanity, the kingdom of the plants also separated from humanity's evolution during the plant phase, taking from man the excessive vital life-force, which would have made it impossible for man's constitution to develop further in order to receive the element of the soul, which was the essence of the animal phase of man. Hence the relationship between the plant form and the human figure. Hence the possibility for us to nourish ourselves with plants. Not only do we take in plant substance in eating vegetables, in digesting a plant, we also experience a relationship with *form*, a form that is the result of the activity of formative forces. These formative forces also work in us, as we have shown. Digestion is, in the first place, an encounter of our body with a form, a structure, the result of creating forces. The result of this encounter is that our physical form is maintained. It is not difficult to understand that the relationship between the human form and the plant is

of equal importance to the understanding of restoring
that form by using herbs when a person falls ill.

The Kingdom of the Minerals and Human Evolution

With the animal we generally feel a strong relationship, especially of course, with the domestic ones living
with us. With plants, there still exists a notable connection in the way we share the vital activity, the growing
and unfolding of the plants in our garden and environment. In caring for and growing plants we come to
understand the expression, to have a green thumb. The
kingdom of the minerals is, so to speak, "farther away" in
the experience of its silence, the impression of its power,
its intense relationship to the forces of gravity. Just as we
have asked with the animal and plant kingdoms, so we
may ask, what does the mineral show, what are its characteristic qualities? We see the animals move and the
plants grow, but the mineral does not show its main physical and chemical qualities without investigation. As it is
our task to understand again how people in ancient times
had such a different conception, not only of plants but
also of mineral substances, we must become acquainted
with the mineral kingdom in a new way as well. What do
we owe the mineral kingdom? In the first place, we owe
to it the possibility of being upright beings. Everyone
knows the joy of feeling firm ground under his feet, especially after he has walked on soft soil such as a sandy
beach. Firm ground supports us in our daily life. Furthermore, technical development would have been impossible without the mineral world. In housing, tools, and the
like, it is the mineral kingdom that provides us with our
needs and enables us to maintain our lives. Finally, we
owe to it our visibility, which, of course, is true for the
other kingdoms as well.

To complete our picture of the unfolding significance of the separation of the kingdoms of nature from human evolution (animals: taking away the superfluous amount of desire; plants: taking away the superfluous amount of vitality), we might add that the mineral kingdom took away man's tendency to densify or materialize too soon in the sequence of evolution. The image of the kingdoms of nature in their relationship to our evolution thus creates a clear composition. This composition allows us to discover a secret that accords with the concept of evolution already given.

We have described the plant as a fully open being, without a "content," as opposed to the animal, which has a soul life limited to sense impressions. As the plant shape consists essentially of lines and surfaces, it is not difficult to accept it as being one on which the environment (water, air, light, and warmth) works from without. This can be expressed in this way: life appears *at* the plant. The animal, with its inward life, can be characterized by saying: the soul appears *in* the animal. About the human being, however, especially when we think of the creative power of humanity, of the fact that man is the only creating being on earth (the animal does not create, it repeats), we are allowed to say: the spirit appears on earth *through* man.

The mineral asks for a different approach. If we imagine a landscape without any living being, we call it a desert. Desert means deserted. (We also sometimes speak of a God-forsaken country.) "Deserted." Does that word not suggest that it is being left alone? Could we not think of a creative principle, a divine reality that "deserted" it? If we call life, soul, and spirit revelations of the divine essence, then the expressions, *at* the plant, *in* the animal, *through* man, may be rounded off with *out of* the mineral. The mineral belongs to a kingdom whose hidden qualities begin to be revealed if the environment offers the possibility.*

Special Minerals in our Environment

There is an important connection between metals and man's life. Each metal has a special character. These characters show themselves, for instance, in the way the metals have appeared in our technology in the course of time.** The nature of iron appears in the use humanity makes of it wherever he is in need of strength in construction (railways, bridges, derricks, reinforced concrete, etc.).

If we think of an illness like anaemia (a well-known example in former times was chlorosis, a primary anaemia, especially of young girls), we know about the notable effect of treatment with iron. The physical appearance of these patients was quite characteristic. They were, of course, very pale but had, above all, lost their typical individual expression. Their gaze was dull, their color greenish: hence the word chlorosis! They were tired, spiritless, as if all energy had disappeared. The influence of iron treatment was striking. In a few weeks the whole picture had changed, together with the fact that

---

*If someone were to ask whether there isn't a similar connection between the inner being of man and the kingdom of minerals to that which we have found between man and the animal and plant kingdoms, the answer could be given in some wonderful expressions that show an interesting relationship between special qualities in our character and the mineral kingdom. I refer to the expressions, an iron will, crystal-clear thinking, a belief that can move mountains, a heart of gold, etc.

**See *Seven Metals* by W. Pelikan (Philosophisch-Anthroposophischer Verlag, Dornach, Switzerland) and *Living Metals* by the author (Regency Press, London).

the healthy color had returned. It is as if we clearly experience the constructive force of that metal in such a case, if given the proper chance. This offers the possibility of considering iron in its specific role in the healthy human constitution. We have seen how the maintenance of our shape has to do with our warmth organization, which is also the bearer of our ego-organization. In this sense the iron serves the ego-organization in its efforts to maintain the human form.

This is only a very simple example. To speak about the character of a metal, we need to study it thoroughly in many of its aspects. We must become really acquainted with the metals (with other mineral substances as well, of course) when trying to discover their proper nature. It is wonderful to experience the fact that a particular mineral substance always speaks the same language!

It is important not to forget the role the mineral world plays in our daily life: man's upright position in connection with the mineral kingdom, and its use in technology, which enables us to maintain our lives; also our visibility, which means that the mineral substances give us the possibility of being physical beings. It is possible to feel the connection between the three examples: maintenance of our uprightness, of our life on earth, and of our living form. Perhaps here the conclusion is justified that the mineral kingdom can be of importance also in the case of illness, if there is a need to reinforce the ego-organization.

The healing, restoring forces, which we dealt with in relation to the Egyptian era, were forces issuing from beings. In the Greek age these beings were considered to belong to the field of activity of high, spiritual beings called Apollo and Mercury. In Greek mythology Mercury often is called the healing god. Aesclepius can be con-

sidered one of the forms in which Mercury appeared.*
The fact that we call Mercury the god of medicine and
that we still use his sign in our medical emblem—the
snake winding round the staff—is a remnant of this ancient wisdom. Why, though, the name Mercury? Mercury is known as a metal. Has this metal anything to do
with the god Mercury?

Mercury, in everyday life, is used in thermometers
and barometers. Many of us may have had the experience
of a broken thermometer and know what fun it was to
play with the strange metal. Many may have pressed on it
with a finger and seen how it expanded into many little
drops that gathered again into one big drop. This is a first
experience with mercury: expanding, contracting. This
quality, however, is discovered only by this experiment.
It is in a way a hidden quality.

Paracelsus, as we have mentioned, applied the word
"Mercury" to the middle ("leafy") part of the plant. It is
Goethe who gave a very characteristic description of the
composition of the plant. He said that at the bottom we
have the large leaves; in the calyx they contract; in the
flower they expand again as petals; in the ovary once
again contraction; in the fruit a third expansion occurs,
followed by a third contraction into the seed. Three times
expansion, three times contraction. This description of
Goethe's metamorphosis of the plant is in harmony with
the conception of Paracelsus. It was Goethe who taught
that, from the root to the top, the plant was, fundamen-

---

*The fact that we hear the same thing about the god Apollo should not confuse
us. In the realm of mythology we have to do with an interplay of many beings.
This highly interesting problem cannot be analyzed in this context.

tally, leaf. We can combine what the two scientists stated by saying that the mercurial element in the plant expresses itself in expansion and contraction, as we have experienced similarly in the metal (see page 73).

Another example of expansion-contraction* from daily life is the human hand. Making a tight fist and then opening the hand wide reveals a corresponding image. This image is not just a random invention. It is very much supported by the fact that our hands are the organs by which man has developed trade or commerce. Commerce means to gather and to divide in a continual alternation. Mercury is also the god of commerce: "commerce" even contains his name. In German, commerce is "Handel," which is directly derived from "hand." We thus can call Mercury the god of our hands.

Why these seemingly playful examples? Because the application of herbs and the laying-on of hands remind us of healing connected with the spiritual world as described in ancient times: three times we are reminded of Mercury.

To find more links to the phenomenon of mercury, we must not forget that the deformative influences in the life-body have been described in connection with the "fall of man." The fall of man was at the same time a fall into matter. The whole of our description of illness over the course of time is a picture of a steadily increasing fall into matter, which ends in a definite separation of humanity from the spiritual world: materialism. Regarding the healing forces, we have often said that they appeared in the form of fever, of warmth. Warmth is a dissolving force; warmth annihilates exactness, even in the world of physics. The tendency of healing, from the beginning,

---

*In German we have the wonderful words "*Ballen und Spreizen*," to form into a ball and to spread.

has always consisted of re-establishing as much as possible the connection of man with his origin, in lifting man out of the intense increase of earthliness, so to speak. On the other hand, this warmth, called fever, is always accompanied by an increase in respiration!

Mercury has other remarkable qualities; it is a metal and, at the same time, a liquid. All metals can be liquefied or melted when they are heated: a liquid metal is, therefore, hot. Mercury is a liquid metal; it should be hot, yet it is not. Alchemists were highly impressed by this quality and described mercury as hiding its warmth, as having a hidden flame. This can be seen in relation to a third surprising quality of mercury: it dissolves other metals. All metals, except iron, dissolve in mercury. It is as if mercury seduces the metals to give up a certain amount of their earthliness. We even feel an inclination to regard mercury as a cosmic metal, but again, this quality is a hidden one! It shows itself only in the practical experiment.

In early times we find the relationship between the seven so-called heavy metals and the seven main organs of the human body:

lead:	spleen
tin:	liver
iron:	gall bladder (a liquid organ)
gold:	heart
copper:	kidneys
mercury:	lungs
silver:	reproductive organs

Modern science generally dismisses this approach as something not deserving attention. My question is, what is the origin of these connections? To call them "fabrications" I would call a fabrication. The only possible answer to me is that we do not know; the only sensible supposition to me is that our consciousness must have changed, as I have tried so often to show. Be that as it may, we hear about a relationship between mercury and the lungs; our lungs are the organs of respiration, inspiring and expiring, expanding and contracting; the qualities are the same as those we have discovered in connection with mercury. The hidden flame, an image of warmth; expanding-contracting, the image of respiration; refusing earthliness, a cosmic tendency: in these three qualities we may recognize the opposite of what we found in cancer: coolness, suffocation, excess of the earthly. It is as if the image of mercury is united with the healing impulse throughout the ages.

Special Plants in our Environment

We have seen that the threefold composition in man may show irregularities in the form of a preponderance at the nerve-sense pole or at the metabolic-limb pole; the plant form may show a preponderance at either the flowering pole, the root pole, or the rhythmic center (the green leafy part). Without going into details of the various forms in which these deviations and disharmonies of the ideal structure of the plant are complicated by other anomalies of the natural life-processes of the plant, it may be understood that one can discover a relationship between special deformations in the human composition and special deformations in the plant shape as a whole.

We may also, by and by, develop a feeling for the intuitive knowledge regarding the plant world that must have existed in the times before Hippocrates, when mystery wisdom was still alive. The difference between

that age and modern times is that then the initiates*
began with a natural openness to what we would call now
the creating forces of the visible plant, because they had
special organs of perception. To them it was compulsory to
find the plant on earth that belonged to their spiritual
perception. We, on the other hand, must begin with the
physical image of the plant and must create new organs of
perception of the supersensible plant being by observing
and studying the visible plant in an appropriate way.

Paracelsus used the expressions, sulfur, mercury, and
salt (sal). He thus indicated the same threefold principle
we find in the plant. He had a spontaneous awareness of
the experiences of former times and at the same time anti-
cipated a way of studying nature in the future. It is as if
nature spoke its secret language to him.

The mystery of restoration, to which we have referred
as healing, has already been explored in the chapter,
"Toward an Extension of Modern Medicine," in the
description of the conversation I held with a colleague
during the second World War. I used the expression, we
must free the world, the truth, from the enchanted form
of the plant. The word, it was said, works on the
construction of the life-body. This would imply, in terms
of its relationship to the kingdom of the plants, that the
human living form was restored or healed by "the Word
of God."

Of course, the healing plant and the deformed life-
body must have certain things in common; there must be a
relationship between the deviation of the herb from the
"normal," healthy plant and the deviation of the life-body
from the healthy life-body! Here, the principle of the

---

*The individuals who lived in direct contact with spiritual beings.

"law" of Hahnemann—*similia similibus curentur* (the same is healed by the same)—is quite justified. This is why we must speak about special deformations in a plant.

While explaining the background of nutrition, we have not yet mentioned that nutritional plants are also "abnormal." By abnormal I mean that practically all plants we use for our nourishment are cultivated. It is not easy to accept the fact that the earth, in its natural condition, cannot feed humanity. Nutritious plants differ from "normal" ones in a very special way. A normal plant, for instance, has its color and its sweetness in the flower as petals and nectar. In this regard, the orange carrot is definitely abnormal, because it has its color and sweetness in the roots. Besides, that root has thickened. It gives the impression that something from the top has been guided downward. We get a similar impression when we look at cabbages. Cabbages are "pushed-down leaves," thicker than normal leaves, more substantial, more juicy. Do we not recognize the same principle in onions, in potatoes, in cauliflowers? Forces of a very special character, carried by the light and warmth of the sun, have been guided downward so that the plant has become "stuffed." The so-called "stuffed plants" contrast with the beautiful plants, which are the plants we have in our gardens, in our rooms, the plants (many of them are also cultivated) that bless our life with beauty; as has been said already, we cannot live without flowers.

In addition to the beautiful plants and the stuffed plants, we have the group of healing plants, the herbs, for which we must find another characteristic. Just as a rose can never be a nutritional plant, so it can never be an herb. As soon as a plant shows the qualities of an herb, of a medicinal plant, something very special begins to characterize it: the fact that it produces some form of poison.

Real herbs are mainly poisonous plants. What is a poison, however? What do we mean if we say a substance is extremely poisonous? I think this means that quite a small quantity can produce a tremendous effect. The smaller the quantity needed to produce a certain effect, the more poisonous the poison is. How do we know that something is a poison? It must be linked with a special experience of life: in the realm of minerals, "to be poisoned" makes no sense. Can we speak of a poisoned plant? Maybe, but it certainly is not an expression often used. In the domain of animal and man the effect of poison shows itself in a most characteristic way. This effect may be explained with the example of a snake-bite.

From descriptions we learn that the moment a person is bitten by a venomous snake, he has the feeling that his body is suddenly permeated by a terrible force, attacking his health, causing pain, anxiety, and the like. It is as if there is an "explosion" inside his body. I think this is the case with each poison in a way. A poison is a substance containing a force that tends to expand into every direction if it is given a chance. We should not forget that the field of expansion is, in this case, the living body of animal or man.

The effect of poison reminds me of the word "agression." Aggression is a typical characteristic of the animal and, of course, also of man, in so far as he has the animal element in him, as we have seen when speaking about evolution and the kingdom of the animals.* The poison-

---

*It is interesting to see that when we find venom in animals, we generally have to do with relatively small animals. To appreciate this law in a proper way we must be very careful in our observations. Mosquitoes, bees, ants are typical examples. The snake is also one, and if someone thinks of the rattlesnake and the cobra as exceptions, he should not forget that in a special way the snake is a very small animal if you do not look at its length but at its height! In short, an elephant cannot be poisonous; he is too large.

ous plant need not necessarily be small; it has, however, another quality that approaches the same principle: it is blocked. Poisonous plants appear to me to be plants in which forces are held back; blockage means to hold something back, as in a state of tension. I hope it has become clear that blockage, tension, aggression, and explosion, taken together, create an overall picture that brings us closer to the mysterious qualities of poison.

In the outline we gave of evolution, the plant phase appears between the mineral and the animal phases. The plant thus stands between mineral and animal, in our diagram as well as in nature. The roots of the plant are set in the earth, its flowers are touching the kingdom of the animals, whether in outer form or in the fact that the flowers are visited by bees and butterflies. The fact that flowers often have an animal-related form is very significant to me. We also should not forget that in the flower the plant stops growing. The flower is a terminal bud. Flowering stops vitality. In the animal we also meet a limited growth. The truly vegetable part of the plant, its green part, shows that typical vitality is revealed only by the plant kingdom. Plant and animal belong to totally separate kingdoms. Is there no transition? If there is, I think it must be found in the poisonous plant. It is as if the poisonous plant shows a certain force, a desire, metaphorically speaking, to enter, as it were, into the kingdom of the animals. The flower, also related to the animal kingdom in a certain way, I would like to describe as inclining toward, a wish for, the animal. Is the moment the butterfly visits—or as the poet says "kisses"—the flower not a kind of satisfaction of this wish? The pictures of chaste wishes in the flower and desires in the poison, taken together with what I said about poison and blockage, gain a new significance. I would like to express it in this way: in the poison lives the desire of the plant to become an animal.

What was it we said about the animal? We came to the conclusion, looking at the relationship between animal and man, that the animal embodies a deformation that otherwise would have become an inhibition for human evolution. We must remind ourselves that we gave the same definition for illness. The illness informs us, so to speak, about the riddle of healing. If illness enables the body to eliminate a deformation in the life-body, the predispositions, what happens if I give a poison, a "desire," the possibility of fulfillment, if I offer a particular plant the possibility of fulfilling a hidden desire—the desire to become an animal by embodying a deformation in man? We then allow the plant to take away the predisposition in such a way that the illness does not have to do it! We have embodied a predisposition, the same thing the illness would have done.

It is clear that the embodiment must be very gentle, so that the body can erase it again. We can think of illnesses that are also embodiments of predispositions that the body can easily throw off. Many acute inflammations fall into this category; the erasure is achieved through the activity we have recognized in fever.

In the following, we will give a succinct illustration of how to heal a predisposition; we will actually face the problem of cancer. We must keep in mind what we have discovered as principal conditions for healing: to embody the predisposition and to restore the disorder in the body as a whole. Restoration must be achieved by a plant that shows characteristics related to those in the "human plant." We must look for a plant that speaks the language, which is understood as an answer to the question asked by the illness itself.

We can imagine a threefold use of substances taken from each of the three kingdoms. A very subtle indication is given in the following examples. The higher animal has in its physical structure, especially in the forms of its organs, much in common with humanity. Animal substances may substitute for the corresponding ones in the human body; here we are dealing mainly with hormones. Apart from substituting, they can also reinforce the weakened structure of some organ. In this case they support the formative activities. The plant gives medicine the possibility of taking away the deformation of the life-body. The mineral supports the ego-organization in rebuilding a complete structure.

The Prospect of Healing Cancer

If we consider all we have learned here about cancer, we might think mercury is the real substance for healing cancer. We have seen that mercury is the substance that bears the cosmic qualities of warmth and respiration—the opposite of cancer—in a hidden way. The picture we have built up regarding the healing of illness, however, and cancer in particular, is different. One of the main points was the relationship between plant and man and the necessity of finding the proper herb that could "speak the proper language" to cure the disease. Mercury certainly has played an important role in medicine of the past. The application of mercury in the case of syphilis is well known. Syphilis is, however, an inflammation, at certain times even an epidemic. In this case, the ego-organization had to be reinforced.

In the case of cancer, we are in need of a substance able to permeate the whole living body with a new impulse and, because of the relationship between plant and

Drawing of mercury drops

Drawing of mistletoe

Photograph of mistletoe in a tree

man, we must look for a plant. If only mercury were a
plant, it would make things easy; it is, however, a metal.
Let us draw some mercury drops. Imagine how we might
turn these mercury drops into a plant. By drawing a
few lines the reader may suddenly feel what we are aim-
ing at.

As we have seen, each plant has mercurial qualities,
but there is a very special plant that shows this quality to
an extreme degree, so much so that we are forced to make
a close study of this plant in order to discover that its
qualities are more mercurial than those of any other plant
in the world. I refer to mistletoe, *viscum album*.

The description of mistletoe reveals the most unexpected characteristics. To begin with, it has a life-cycle
bearing no relationship with the life-cycle of other plants.
The plant, on the whole, is a seasonal being, as everyone
knows. Mistletoe has no regard for seasons. It does not
care from which direction the light comes; scientifically
speaking, it is neither a positive nor a negative photo-
trope. It never grows on the earth but always on other
plants, mainly on trees. In summertime, the plant can
hardly be seen, as it grows in the dark part of the tree, inside the foliage; in wintertime, it is clearly seen in the
crown of many trees. The mistletoe bushes are round;
hence the similarity to drops of mercury. They are green:
leaves, stalks, seeds, and roots. Everything is extremely
green. Green, however, is the mercury part of the plant,
as Paracelsus called it. This green color deepens during
summer when mistletoe lives in the dark. In wintertime,
when mistletoe is more exposed to the light, the green
turns slightly yellowish. It is as if mistletoe, in being exposed to the sun, says, "I have not forgotten you; I carry
you within myself." This turning yellow can indeed be
looked at as a flourishing of the whole plant; it has

nothing to do with a withering away. As long as the tree on which it grows is alive, mistletoe remains alive.

Most remarkable is mistletoe's structure; from afar it looks like a round ball; nearby we discover the characteristic ramifications, which are called dichotomic, as can be seen in the illustration:

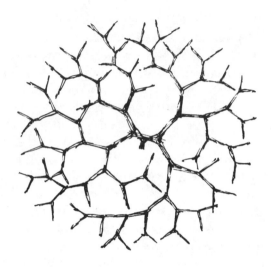

Drawing of the ramifications of mistletoe

This construction is very much like the ramifications of the bronchial ducts in the lungs. We need not wonder that mistletoe and the lungs are both called mercurial.

What is important is that this dichotomic, lung-related structure is not visible from afar: it can be discovered only by close examination. The relationship of mistletoe to the sun must be discovered too, by studying the plant in its dark or light color; there is no obvious, clear connection with the sun. We can come to the conclusion that in mistletoe, as in mercury, we find "hidden respiration" and "hidden warmth." The fact that mistletoe takes no notice of the seasons is also something that must be taken into account. We can speak of a hidden dislike for the earth. I have emphasized the word "hidden" three times.

In the last section we dealt with the healing plant, the herb, and said that herbs could be seen as stagnated or blocked plants. In the chapter, "Toward an Extension of Modern Medicine," the expression "language of the plant" was used for the first time. "Blockage," "hidden," "language": can we not find a connection among these three conceptions? The herb has been called a plant with a desire, something that does not live in a normal plant. The normal plant, a beautiful plant, a "plant to look at," reveals itself, "lives itself out"; it is not blocked. It may speak to our imagination, but this is something different from speaking in the sense of the "language of the herb." Here we have to do with a hidden herb force which, because of the blockage, is still "unpronounced." That is why mistletoe can speak in a threefold way to the ego-organization of the cancer patient in a language of which it is in need. Proceeding along these lines may bring us closer to perceiving mistletoe as the specific medicine for cancer.*

Two things may be clear: firstly, we have discovered a new possibility for approaching the secret living behind the form of the plant. In ancient times, as we have seen, herbs were known, but it is not clear how they were found. Certainly not by way of experiments, as the

---

*To give more details about cancer treatment is not the aim of this book. I will limit myself to the information that several hundreds of doctors from around the world, continually increasing in number, have been trying this new treatment for cancer for some decades already. The center is the "Lukas Klinik" in Arlesheim (Switzerland), where doctors and students are trained as well.

sources of wisdom came from spiritual contact. This relationship to the spiritual world gradually diminished and finally disappeared. We have already spoken of man's instinctive relationship to the creating beings of the plant. Now our approach is the opposite one: we start from the physical shape of the plant, looking at it in such a way that we can experience the composition, so as to come to a new relationship with the "composer." This path of gaining new knowledge will, of course, have to be supported by the development of many more qualities of the human soul.

Secondly, we should understand that this is, at the same time, an answer to the doctor's question in the conversation I have so often mentioned: "Do you know the language of God?" If,however, this is the beginning of knowing how to speak that language again, our newly developed conception of healing bears evidence of it.

What is the situation in the medical world? Medicine today is proud of its achievements, and we cannot deny them. The moment doctors claim to be able to heal inflammations by antibiotics, however, I must warn against rash statements. From the beginning we have called healing a restoration of the form. Do antibiotics restore that form? Not in the least. The form is restored by the very forces that are denied by modern science, the *creating* forces. The nearest recognition of such a healing force is the expression: *vis medicatrix naturae.* What is the effect of antibiotics? They take away or attack the symptom of inflammation. A Dutch professor of internal medicine* has stated:

> They are not always used in a favorable way; one should not give patients suffering from pneumonia antibiotics

*Dr. G. Borst, Amsterdam.

from the start. It is better if they have a high fever for a certain length of time.

It seems rather a paradox, although necessary, to make the remark that inflammations heal by themselves. We can only guide them; we certainly do have to guide them, accepting the use of antibiotics in some cases. The fact that these are not truly healing substances, the fact that medicine has indeed forgotten what healing in reality means, as was my point at the outset, is illustrated by the fact that the moment this self-healing of the body is no longer evident, the moment doctors are not dealing with inflammations, modern medicine has no possibility of healing whatsoever. The achievements in treating destructive, degenerative illnesses can never be called healings, much as we may admire or make use of these treatments. I pointed out already that in all illnesses like cancer, heart and vessel diseases, rheumatic diseases, and diseases of the central nervous system, we have no possibility of healing, only of helping, of fighting symptoms, and, at the utmost, awaiting the self-healing of the body. As for substances in modern medicine that are taken from the animal kingdom, hormones in particular, we should be careful to observe that these substances also never bring about healing. They are substitutes; they can save lives, as we have seen in the case of diabetes, but healing is something different, as may have become clear.

The understanding of the fundamental contrast between inflammation and cancer leads to a better attitude of man toward fever and warmth. Too often we come upon a medical attitude that has little or no understanding at all for fever. "Fever is illness"; that is all one hears. This error has far-reaching consequences, as doctors have not hesitated to prescribe and favor medicines that decrease temperature and so diminish our warmth. We should be aware of the fact that nearly all pain-killers, also many tranquillizers and sleeping tablets, tend to lower our temperature, although hardly noticeably. If, on the other hand, we were to develop a sympathy for warmth, foreseeing that our ego-organization is based on our warmth organization, we would be more careful with prescriptions in relevant cases. Humanity tends to lose its respect for warmth. "Our warmth is in danger" is not an empty saying.

Now the right moment has come to give careful consideration to a rather delicate subject. It is well known that a cancer patient also can develop an inflammatory illness. (I remember a striking case of a woman with a sarcoma, a special form of cancer, who contracted an erysipelas, an inflammation of the skin with very high fever). When this occurs the cancer condition improves for the time being. I think each doctor will know of such a case. In our time, however, a doctor may overlook the importance of this phenomenon. He may say to himself, and perhaps even also to the patient, "The tumor I cannot heal, but I can at least take away the inflammation, because we have antibiotics." If he took a broader view, he definitely would not underestimate the favorable influences of the fever.

This is the situation when the cancer patient develops an inflammation. Another possibility is that a person has an inflammation some time before a cancer develops. Is it not possible to feel that the inflammation, causing a reconstruction of the life-body, definitely works in favor of decreasing the chance of developing cancer? If this is so, should we not remind ourselves that inflammations balance, as it were, the cancer tendency? I do not mean to say that they always can prevent cancer, but inflammation, no doubt, will always counteract to some extent the cancer tendency.

Cancer is an illness of maturity. Inflammations, on the other hand, belong primarily to youth. If we look at life as a whole, studying youth and age in relationship to one another, should we not consider whether it is right to regard inflammations and cancer as if they were the same? Is it correct to fight children's illnesses as if they were catastrophes like cancer, as if they were epidemics of the Middle Ages, when the "scourge of God" killed one third of the population of Europe? This is what the medical profession tries to convince us of: "We should fight measles, chickenpox, whooping cough, and so on, those terrible epidemics that tend to destroy the greater part of our youth."

This is propaganda. "Let us try to get rid of the measles because it is a bother," was the expression used in an article in a medical periodical in 1978. This shows how measles is regarded. Of course, in every illness, even in the most innocent one, there may be exceptions. During my life as a practitioner from 1930 to 1970, I treated thousands of children during epidemics of all the common children's illnesses. I witnessed the time when it became common practice to fight off whooping-cough by vaccination. I even treated babies with whooping-cough, which is said to be lethal in many cases. Never did I lose any child to one of these illnesses. I fear we must remind ourselves of the influence of economics in the realm of medicine.

Here I would like to inform the reader of another error that has become solidly rooted in public opinion. It is the fear of pneumonia. It is the general opinion that if pneumonia is not treated with antibiotics the patient will probably die. Going back to the 1920's, I remember how our professor taught us about the prognosis for pneumonia. Babies under a year, aged people over seventy, and hunchbacks are endangered, we were informed. A healthy person, however, generally overcomes pneumonia.* I think this information illustrates my original point, that inflammations are illnesses that principally heal by themselves, even if someone might contradict this, saying he has a different impression of the danger of pneumonia.

Propaganda, public opinion, play a large role. I believe that most doctors striving for elimination of children's illnesses are convinced that they do a great service. At the same time, I myself am convinced that medical science should be very careful not to be blind, not to exaggerate where it makes no sense, not to throw out the baby with the bath-water; and above all, it must keep an eye on the hidden danger of falling unknowingly into the trap of economics. To me, children's illnesses should be treated in the proper way, by supporting the illness in its effort to restore the form, not fighting the illness. On the other hand, we should consider them as the greatest blessings, because through them man is able to strengthen his personal form by conquering a predisposition, enabling him to incarnate better. To me it is beyond doubt that the increase in cancer is *partly* a result of the elimination of the inflammatory illnesses, especially the children's illnesses.

No one should draw the conclusion that I mean to advise stopping all vaccination. In my long practice I was, of course, confronted with this problem; as long as medicine has not yet developed the ability to treat life-threatening illnesses in an appropriate way, vaccination will, for most people, be the only way out. My intention is to show the possibility of a new approach in the future.

---

*Here we must make an exception for the cases during the flu epidemic of 1918. As we have seen, however, this can be understood only against the background of the time in which it took place.

An illustration of the awareness of the importance of warmth can be seen in new treatments of cancer, the so-called "heat treatments." For several years already we have heard of cancer patients being treated with hot baths, often baths that were so hot that the patient had to be put under total anaesthesia. Whether these applications are done in the right way is not our main concern. The question is whether the thought itself is logical, healthy, and creative. Only the future will reveal this. Modern medicine was characterized in the section, "Anti-forces," as "violent," in spite of all its good intentions, and we as well should be careful not to fall into violence. Violence should be transformed into dedication; to speak the language of the formative forces requires a very special approach.

Illness takes away the predisposition that originates in the life of the soul. By eliminating the predisposition, as we have seen, man is allowed to live better in his body; we even used the expression that man can continue on his path. We have annihilated a blockage. There are, however, many illnesses in which we do not encounter the phase in which man is able to eliminate his predisposition during his life; these are illnesses that last until death. On the other hand, we meet many cases in which a person is clearly born with a predisposition. The question may be posed, if there has been no soul life before birth, how was the predispositon caused by problems of the soul, and, if there is no life after death, in what respect does the extension of the illness until the moment of death make sense?

This problem was mentioned when we considered whether birth and death are either the beginning and end of man's existence or the gates through which we pass. We have reached the moment to begin a new exploration, the background of man's biography.

Changing Our Minds

*The Course of Human Life: A Consideration of
Reincarnation*

We have already seen that the person who stands
before us is a complicated being. The individuality we
have referred to as the "I" or ego is so strongly connected
with the personality and again so strongly connected with
the living body, especially in highly cultivated Western
countries, that we tend to identify our "I" or ego (spirit)
with the personality (soul) and the body.

Considering the sum of man's life we come to the conclusion that our previous thoughts about the predisposition, the taking away of the predisposition, the significance of illness and healing, are all irrelevant if we are
unable to find access to a concept without which life appears to me to have no meaning: I am talking about the
idea of reincarnation.

Many will say that they do not believe in reincarnation. Reincarnation can, however, be considered as a possibility. In that case we can accept it as an idea; whether
this idea satisfies us or not is another issue. We may
discover that our experiences in the field of illness, of
healing, of everything we have taken into consideration,
will strengthen, enhance, support that idea. Here I wish
to add that in my opinion reincarnation cannot be proved.
We continually meet people and come upon societies or
methods by which people try to prove reincarnation. To
me all this is illusory. It would be proof only if we were
able consciously to follow a person during his life after
death until rebirth. This is impossible, at least without appropriate organs of perception, as we discussed in the section about evolution.

If we try to examine the concept of reincarnation, it is
necessary to discuss and discover to which element in

man reincarnation could be relevant. We know our body by physical perception. Our inward soul life, to which we refer as our personality, we know from memory. Memory, however, is connected with the past and future, realms of time.* An interesting fact reveals itself: our body is connected with space, and our soul (or personality) is connected with time. There is, however, another principle, a third principle that *has* a body and *is* called by a particular name but that goes beyond space and time. The concept "eternity" comes to meet us as a reality beyond space and time. It is a fascinating thought that, in spite of the fact that we cannot imagine eternity as we can imagine elements in space and time, we can nevertheless conclude that something beyond space and time must exist in man. This is the consequence of the fact that we can speak *about* space and time, that we possess concepts of space and time, for we can speak about matters only if in some way or other we are facing them. A Dutch professor, De Vroe, once gave an excellent illustration of this law by explaining that a fish swimming in water does not "know" the water. To stress his assertion he continued, "Only on the kitchen table—outside the water does the fish gain the possibility of knowing water."

This also explains why I spoke about the identification of ego, personality, and body, which have been scarcely distinguished in the cultivated Western countries. Especially the English-speaking peoples, the Germans, and the Dutch have achieved an ego-identification. If asked, "Who are you?" the usual answer is, "I am . . ., *Ich Bin . . ., ik ben . . .*" If, on the other hand, a Frenchman is asked the same question, he would, in many cases,

*If we make plans for tomorrow, we move about on the same level as our memory did yesterday.

answer, "I call myself . . ." (*"Je m'appelle"*). In Italy we find the same, *"Mi chiamo . . ."* In Hungary, when asking someone's name, one says; "How do they call you?" These examples illustrate an awareness of the difference between the I or ego and the personality. The experience of this difference has gradually disappeared in the West, and this is one of the reasons that people have difficulty acknowledging that part in them to which the idea of reincarnation applies.

A little story may illustrate this point. Long ago, during an evening festivity, an elderly lady addressed me in a loud voice over the heads of many people, "Aren't you the doctor who believes in reincarnation?" As I understood what she meant, I could only agree. "Well," she said more or less jokingly, "I would only like to inform you that I definitely do not even wish to come back." In return I said, "Don't be afraid, my lady, you won't come back." Surprisingly, she got a little angry and said, "Oh, but *you* are coming back, aren't you?" "No," I said, "I won't come back either."

This touches on the point that when speaking about reincarnation we have, first of all, to analyze man in such a way that we can discover that special element in him to which the concept of reincarnation is applicable. When someone says, "I will come back," he forgets that he is identifying his "*I am*" with his personality. We make a mistake if we say, for example, "Goethe reincarnated." Goethe never lived before and will never live again: he lived only once as Goethe; his Goethe-incarnation is unique. What gives me information about Goethe himself? His biography. The biography reveals the earthly garment in which the eternal aspect of man is clothed. How does the biography come into being? It develops through experiences of life. Continually we meet people and, of course, events. What does it mean, "to meet"? One quality can easily be overlooked: meeting always happens by chance. If we meet someone not by chance, it is not a meeting but a visit. We speak of having met someone when we did not expect to see him. Here another word is introduced: chance. What does the expression "by chance" imply? When do we say "something happens by chance"? Only if it is in some way surprising and if it has some significance for us. To have significance means at the same time that it has some relationship to us, that there is some connection between the event and us. This leads to an unexpected conclusion: meetings happen by chance, but "by chance" is always a kind of meeting. Meeting includes a connection. We have taken one more step: a biography is built up of meetings by chance, of coincidental meetings.

I would like to give illustrations of this relationship. If someone is musical, we can recognize his musicality only in connection with an instrument. If someone feels sympathy for someone else in his environment, this sympathy can show itself only when he meets that person. If someone has a predisposition for an illness, e.g., scarlet fever, this predisposition can show itself only when that person "meets" another case of scarlet fever.

In the first example, we speak of talent, in the second of sympathy, in the third of predisposition. The reader will recognize that we have dealt with this subject in the section about predisposition for an illness. I always have an inclination to speak of a talent, not only in the case of an illness but also in the case of sympathy between two persons. To have a talent for an instrument, a talent for a person, and a talent for an illness unites the three examples in the word "talent." We might say that man is born with innumerable talents, if we apply the word to all coincidental meetings. A talent literally means a weight; people were paid in talents of silver in earlier times. We will come back to this fact later.

What is the significance of those talents in the course of life? They contribute to the development of the biography. Life consists partly of displaying innumerable talents in ever-so-many meetings with people and situations in the course of time. The biography, however, consists not only of meetings but also of answers, actions, and deeds of the person concerned. That which reveals itself after birth, creating all the situations we meet, along with our answers and reactions to those situations, builds up our biography.

At the end of his life, man looks back over all his memories that sum up, so to speak, his whole biography, the sum of all the events that happened and all the deeds he performed. Yet there is still more. Every discussion I have had, everything I have done, has two sides to it: it is stored in my memory and also in that of the person concerned. We very often do not know what happens to the impressions we make on our environment. We may remember how frequently a little something, a word or a gesture, is of great consequence. One word can change a whole life. These effects we generally lose from sight. During his life man leaves behind him a track of all his deeds. These impressions on the environment, we said just now, can be lost from sight, but they maintain a certain relationship to us; they bear the imprint of our personality. When man has arrived at the end of his life, there are two elements that must be distinguished: one is the content of his biography, the other is the sum of all the imprints that live in other persons but that have been lost from sight.

The question arises, however: couldn't it be that the relationships that arise from his talents have in some way

to do with the relationship between the man and the
tracks that he lost from sight? Are these talents, of which
we spoke just now, not a result of relationships created in
a former life?

As we saw, a talent was originally a weight. The force
of gravity attracts something toward the earth. Would it
be possible to suggest that a subtle, hidden attraction is
expressed in this relationship? This is just a query. I think
it more helpful to ask a question than to give an inappro-
priate answer. It will only be fruitful to look and see
whether we do have experiences in life that support the
thought we are dealing with. For example, nearly everyone has experienced meeting some person who knew
some other person whom he also knew and saying, "Isn't
it a small world?" My answer is, "No, the world is enormously large, but the group of people who are intimately
related is certainly relatively small."

What happens to our talents during life? The talents
for people are "lived out." The talents that show themselves in professions are "worked out"; the talents that we
have called predisposition disappear through illness: This
means, consequently, that illness, as part of man's biography, can truly be accepted if we do not look at man's
life as being limited to the span between birth and death.
Let us not forget that a predisposition indicated a deformation, a blockage. In recovering from an illness, man is
able to overcome this blockage; he can continue on his
way.

The questions can arise, what does it matter if man
simply eliminates his symptoms in the case of an illness?
Why should man not be able to fulfill his life just as well
if he has no more complaints? What objection could be
made to the modern way of treatment? Is not an illness
indeed senseless?

The answer must be a very delicate one. Man can certainly live with a body treated in such a way that he is filled with substances that suppress symptoms and complaints. Our concern has never been with humanity's ability to live but with its ability to evolve. As soon as man's existence is considered to be limited by birth and death, illness is definitely—as has been said already—senseless. The moment we develop a totally new conception of life, not separated from the conception of evolution—which in reality means moral evolution—the possibility of falling ill appears in a new light. Illness is not senseless any longer but becomes a link in man's evolution. Man creates predispositions; illness blesses him by continually taking away the predisposition. Healing, what we have called healing, signifies creating a new lifespan in so far as we have been able to take over the task of the illness.

We have not yet dealt with the problem of inherited illnesses; they too must be considered in the light of reincarnation. We have called the predisposition a talent. Let us consider for a moment the so-called inherited talents. Can a talent really be inherited? Many people will say that they have seen it happen many times. Of course, one receives that impression. Many talented people appear in a single family line. There is another explanation, however, that a talent in itself, as a quality of the individuality, can never be inherited, and yet talented people appear over generations.

We have to do with the fact that not only is the talent a soul quality but it very often also has a close connection with a physical quality. The physical hands of a musician, his "musical" ears, are different indeed from those of anyone else. These physical qualities are transmittable. Let us suppose that an individual bears the intention (here we meet the principle of karma) of becoming a

musician. He will—the reader may excuse the somewhat
simple expression—be searching for the appropriate
body. If, in a special case, parents and their ancestors can
offer a highly adequate body for musicians, we might imagine a real queueing up in the spiritual world. The Bach
family is an excellent example of this inclination.

The problem becomes even more acute when we
think of inherited illnesses, for this would mean that an
individuality would incarnate himself where he might
find the environment through which a special illness
could be "acquired." This would imply that illness must
make sense, which indeed has been suggested repeatedly.

I know how much resistance such an idea will evoke.
It would, at the same time, subvert all efforts being made
to prevent unfavorable inheritances. We must not forget,
however, that though it is true that illness can be considered as a unique solution to the problem of ridding
oneself of a predisposition, we have already seen that this
must be taken in an imaginative way. The laws that lead
to an illness are so complicated that it is quite possible to
provoke an illness to such an extent that an illness can appear in a different way from what would have been the
case if people had not been so reckless. We may even
understand that actually nearly everyone has in principle
some predisposition to illness. We have given the example
of the little cloud in the sky. Circumstances can work so
unfavorably that to say the illness was "provoked" is not
an empty phrase. Besides, we have already understood
that our conception of illness and predisposition does not
exclude influences from without. If someone is a heavy
smoker and develops lung cancer, we have accepted the
fact that the predisposition had to exist first. Whether this
was a predisposition to cancer from the beginning is quite
another story. Smoking, as well as psychosomatic cir-

cumstances, may intensify the predisposition in such a way that cancer is the result. The law still holds that cancer in itself remains a symptom, whereas the predisposition is in fact the real site of the illness.

Experiences in Daily Life

During my practice as a physician I have had several experiences of which I should like to give some examples. These examples contain elements that show a different approach to medical problems from the usual one. Perhaps they may be considered as illustrations of the new way of thinking in the realm of medicine, which was the original point of this book.

Case I

A lady came to me with a rather common complaint. "My heart troubles me." Generally, in such a case, people expect some medicine, some drug, to eliminate their complaints. Though I was seeing her for the first time, her whole behavior compelled me to answer, "I rather have the impression that *you* are troubling your heart."

I was rather surprised at her enthusiastic reaction. She felt, as she said, as if a wrong thought of hers had been corrected. To give a prescription for heart trouble so that the patient is content is certainly possible, justifiable, and, indeed, she too had expected some medicine. At the same time, however, she saw the other side of the story: our body is not merely something that should not trouble us. It is something more, which can best be expressed by calling it a musical instrument. This image evokes our two-sided problem: the instrument and the person who plays it. Healing could also be considered as tuning, but tuning is not sufficient: not only has the artist to obey the laws of his instrument but he himself must also improve and practice a lot in order to play better! I think that putting the problem in this way will teach us to be very careful not to abuse the instrument, meaning the human body, and to be awake to man's responsibility for the moral side of his life.

Case II

Now and then it happens that a patient speaks with a very soft voice, perhaps a little hoarse, perhaps a little shy. Having some difficulty in understanding him or her I have often said suddenly, "Please put some more iron into your voice."

Now I could give a more acceptable and even more-or-less attractive explanation of this expression. I could elaborate on the relationship between our larynx and the forces of "Mars," of which ancient science knew and which was handed down to us. I could try to explain that from the past we are informed about the connection between the god Mars and the metal iron; I could, well, I could say many more things so as to try to justify such an expression. Interestingly enough, however, I have never met anyone who did not understand immediately what I meant. The reaction was always a smiling consent and an agreement to do one's best.

Case III

Other examples with which I have often been confronted are sensitive, nervous persons, sensitive especially to sense impressions (light, noise), restless types, talking a lot, elaborating on details, etc. Here I have often given a

form of educational advice, "You are too much of a butterfly; you should develop the cow element in you more."*

Here again it would not be difficult to show the relationship between the threefold human shape (as has been
considered in the section on healing) and the concepts of
eagle, lion, and bull, which we meet in the image of the
Sphinx, representing the parts of the primeval human being. We encounter the same images in the so-called Apoc-
alyptic beasts that have been related to the writers of the
Gospels. The eagle (the bird) represents our nerve-sense
system, the bull (the cow) our metabolic-limb system; the
lion our rhythmic system, the chest. Without going into
any details, however, all such patients understood immediately what I meant and thus we could go on talking
about their problems, enriched with another characteristic element in the diagnosis.

What do we learn from these examples? That in every
one of us there lives the possibility of looking at the world
in a different way from that which we have built up in the
course of modern education. This new approach asks for a
certain "movement of the soul," consisting of freeing the
soul, be it only for a moment, from fixed prejudices (we
could even speak of paradigms**), which tend to make our
thinking rigid. We experience in such a moment a feeling
of joy. Hence the smiling assent of my patients.

Case IV

A mother called me to come to her child who had high
fever. I gave a quick examination and began to have a

---

*In fact, I said, "You are too much of a bird." If someone has ever seen the way
in which a sparrow or a canary picks at his food, continually looking up and
around, one can understand that with the word "bird" is meant hypersensi-
tivity.

**See *Medicine on a Dead Track* by H. Verbrugh, 1976.

short conversation on the child's state of health. She interrupted me, saying, "But Doctor, we must not waste time; why don't you do anything?" My answer was, "What do you expect me to do? So much is happening already!" I explained to her about fever in the way I have described it in this book.

Case V

Another mother urgently called me because her child had high fever and seizures. Now, if anyone has ever seen a child with a seizure, he can imagine that there is indeed reason for anxiety! She asked me whether I would agree to consult a pediatrician in this case, which of course I did. The specialist was an elderly lady, who came into the room, looked for a moment at the child, took the blanket, uncovering the child completely, then walked with me into another room to discuss what there was to be done. I was somewhat surprised and asked, "Won't the boy catch a cold? She laughed and said, "How can anyone with a high fever catch a cold? His body is fully active. The boy is rather suffering from congestion."

The reader will recognize that here was someone who had, out of a long life of experience, discovered the same truth that we have discussed. At the same time she showed that high fever should be lowered simply by taking away the excess cover. Fever can also be lowered by giving cool compresses on the head or around the calves, and we see that it is not always necessary to use antipyretics or antibiotics.

Case VI

Many patients come with inflammations on arms or legs, often caused by incorrect treatment of small wounds. If a wound, be it a cut or a sting, is covered too quickly with a scab, the immediate danger, which every doctor will have experienced in his practice, is development of a so-called lymphangitis. The spot itself often swells considerably, the surrounding tissues become red, and flame-like stains radiate from it. Often, the lymph glands in the axilla or groin are swollen. The immediate help for this is wet compresses, without interruption, refreshed every time the cloth begins to dry. Water, water.

In cases of high fever, we have also seen that cold-water compresses on the forehead and around wrists or calves give an immediate and great relief. The reason for this is not so difficult to determine: fire must be extinguished. It was amusing to experience the speed by which this expression spread in the town in which I practiced, after someone had passed it on. This was due to the feeling that this was at the same time the revelation of a law from another field of knowledge, differing from that of our everyday routine. It was not the advice itself that was important; there was again the kind of joy you could feel in the hearts of those concerned at experiencing something new, unknown.

Case VII

I became a doctor in a family with many children. One of them, a girl of sixteen, was under the treatment of a specialist, as she suffered from advanced consumption. One day the mother told me that the girl also wished to be treated by me. The specialist (it was still long before antibiotics appeared) had already agreed, considering correctly that she might not have long to live, as her case offered no hope. During the first visit the girl told me that she suffered greatly from being encouraged the whole day to eat. She was skin and bones, as one can imagine, lack of appetite being one of the main symptoms of her illness; she was told all day long, if only she would eat some more, she would gain forces to build up some resistance. My first words were, "Now listen carefully; from this moment on you need not eat anything more than you wish." I will never forget this moment. She began to cry, to cry for joy and happiness! I do not remember how long she lived afterward, some months at least, but these months were free of any persuasion to eat. The end was touching: one evening she asked her parents to lift her up, high up to the ceiling. Then she waved good-bye with her little hand and died.

I have not told this story for sentimental reasons, or for the part I played in it, but I have the feeling that the story indicates something very important. People who are ill generally (we will not consider rare exceptions) lose their appetites. Those around an ill person often try to persuade the patient to eat, to gain forces, just as in the story above. This is quite logical, looked at from nearby; there is no reason to object. Let us consider for a moment, however, that the person is ill; his whole body is permeated by illness. What he eats will become *him*, but as *he* is ill, the more he eats the more there is of him to become ill. That is why "nature" is so wise and makes man eat little or nothing when he is ill.

Case VIII

Another example may reveal still more of the problem with which we are dealing here. A mother came to me with a boy of about ten, who indeed was as thin as a needle. She was afraid that in case of an illness, he might show too little resistance. Could I possibly give him more appetite? I asked the boy, "How do you feel?" "Fine, Doctor," was his answer. "Well," I said to the mother, "Then the only possibility is for you to persuade him to eat more!" "Well," she said, a little irritated, "He doesn't want to!" "Well," I said a little irritated too, "Then don't ask me!" And off she went; I did not lose her as a patient, though. Later on she understood what I meant.

It has long since become general knowledge that thin people are by no means more vulnerable to influences from without than anyone else.

Case IX

There is a certain illness, called Bürger's disease, characterized by gradual deterioration of the arteries, mainly the peripheral ones, especially in feet and legs. Some cases were clearly connected with a soldier's life in the trenches, hence the expression, trench foot. In case of an "attack," these vessels contract very tightly and temporarily inhibit the bloodstream completely. The foot becomes snow-white, icy cold, and the pain must be one of the most horrible to imagine. What would anyone do spontaneously? Put the foot in warm water, in hot water, in something that might enlarge the vessels, which is warmth. Strangely enough, however, this never showed any real effect, nothing did, until someone had the idea of putting the foot in ice! I myself have been able to apply this treatment in practice, and the result was so striking that I could hardly believe. it. The pain vanished instantly! We pondered over what was going on, what could be wrong with warmth and right with cold? By cold treatment, by putting the foot on ice, we were creating externally what the afflicted body was creating internally as a disease. It was as if by our application of ice, the body, or something in the body, was relieved from the unnatural activity, so that it was able to return to its normal condition. We had taken over the wrong activity, so to speak. This description is anything but exact, but, as has been said so often, life, the living body, is never exact.

If we feel that the aforementioned experience should be expressed in a law, this law could be: try to take over that which the ill body shows. This is the case also for the application of a deformed plant to a deformed life-body, as we have shown previously, using the expression, *similia similibus curentur!* We can look at the homeopath, Hahnemann, as someone who discovered by intuition something extending in its importance far beyond his own comprehension of the method.

A second, interesting example of the same principle is the application of gynergen (a derivative of the so-called ergot, a parasite fungus living on the ear of the rye) in a case of migraine. This treatment does not bring a cure, but it helps immediately if given right at the beginning of the attack. Classic migraine begins with typical pre-symptoms; sudden "empty" spots (often making the impression of a "glittering" water-surface) in the field of vision—the so-called scotomes—by which especially the central vision is disturbed. There is no trace of headache then, however. This "blindness" disappears after perhaps a quarter of an hour; shortly after, the real migraine begins. The explanation of this interesting phenomenon lies in the fact that a migraine attack is accompanied by a strong contraction in the small vessels, beginning in the peripheral realm, in the eye, and gradually wandering to the center, until it reaches the brain, where it manifests itself in a headache. Gynergen also causes an immediate, strong contraction of the peripheral blood vessels, similar to what takes place spontaneously in the migraine attack.

The similarity between these two examples is, in my opinion, obvious and opens a new possibility for understanding in the field of treatment and healing.

Case X

The following episode was very instructive to me. A woman consulted me about her husband, who suffered from heart trouble. His legs were swollen, and he suffered from edema due to lack of circulation in his legs. She asked me whether I could explain this to her. To my own astonishment, I heard myself say, "You see, in a way we could say that swollen legs are not unnatural. The water in them runs down. As a matter of fact, water is always running down in nature. We could perhaps put it the other way around by saying that if someone does *not* have swollen legs, it is unnatural!" I continued. "There is more that supports this point of view. In chemistry, calcium has a tendency to precipitate. If in our bodies, for instance in arteriosclerosis, we discover precipitation of calcium, this is quite a natural phenomenon. If the calcium does *not* precipitate, it is unnatural. Another example is coagulation of blood. If we take some blood from a body, it always coagulates. Coagulating is a normal quality of the blood. If the blood does not coagulate in the body, we should marvel and understand that something is preventing it from coagulating, just as something prevents my calcium from precipitating, just as something prevents my 'water' from running down. It is clear that something works in our bodies, something like an anti-chemistry, an anti-physics."

This example can reveal something very special to us, the feeling that we should not regard the processes in living nature as we regard them in the mineral world. It makes us aware that in these cases (the list of which could, of course, be extended) something has lost its grip on processes in us, which now begin to follow laws in nature. It is clear that we are again dealing with the activity of the life-body.

Case XI

Here is a last example to test our flexibility. In the body we have principally two sorts of glands. A number of them (i.e., salivary glands, liver, kidneys, sudory glands, etc.) have ducts by which they "pour" or discharge their products of excretion from the system, be it in the cavity of the intestines, the bladder, or directly onto the surface of the skin (e.g., sweat). A number of different glands have no "ducts"; they are called "ductless" glands, producing substances secreted directly into the blood itself, substances well known as "hormones." Some of these glands are the hypophysis, the thyroid and parathyroid glands, the suprarenal glands, the sexual glands, a part of the pancreas, etc. Many illnesses are known to stand in close relationship to wrong functioning (dysfunction) of one or some of these. A well-known example is diabetes, having to do with a dysfunction of the ductless part of the pancreas.* The functions of all these ductless glands, however, communicate with one another. The function of what is also called the inner secretory part of the pancreas is considered to be controlled by the suprarenal glands, which means that dysfunction of the pancreas originates in those suprarenal glands.

This was, at one time, the opinion of scientific investigators. Later, however, many more relationships were

---

*The pancreas has an excreting glandular part in addition to ductless cell-groups.

discovered. The superrenal glands in their turn were "controlled" by the hypophysis. Some people went so far as to say that all diseases in connection with ductless glands found their main origin in a dysfunction of the hypophysis; this was, so to speak, the beginning point. The latest discovery went still further: the dysfunction of the hypophysis is not the real beginning point; for this we must look to a certain part of our brain, the so-called hypothalamus.

It is obvious that we have only moved the problem, putting it at the end of a number of problems that need to be solved. If at the end there stands again a similar, unsolved problem, however, this is no solution at all, for the question arises, what causes the dysfunction of the hypothalamus? It is clear that in this way we will never be able to come to a real "origin." To do this would be possible only if we were to shift our consciousness to another level, that level out of which the sum of all ductless glands is organized! This means that we must leave the domain of the results and enter the domain of the creating activities themselves. We have called this the domain of the life-body.

The effort we experience in changing our mind in this respect makes thoughts and feelings mobile, which have long been "frozen" in the depths of our souls.

Conditions for Healing in the Future

When we discern the tendencies living in modern medicine, we detect three ideals:

1) To make doctors superfluous;
2) To standardize the medicines;
3) To heal all patients, without the patient having to play any part in it.

I do not think these expressions ask for any further explanation. The term "superfluous" was used by a friend of mine many years ago. "We should make ourselves superfluous," was his enthusiastic comment. To make the doctor superfluous lives as an inclination in the so-called "computer medicine." The standardizing of medicines is closely connected with the well-known "double-blind" proof: patients are given real medicines as well as placebos (imitations) so as to determine whether a medicine is effective or not. It is called double-blind because neither doctor nor patient has any knowledge of what is given.

The conclusions in this book differ considerably from these attitudes:

1) The effect of the medicine is highly dependent on the personality of the doctor;
2) The quality and choice of medicines are continually changing and developing;
3) The possibility of healing depends not only on the doctor and medicine but, just as important, on the patient himself.

Let us begin with the last point. Originally, healing did not depend on the patient at all. Healing was impersonal. Times have changed, however. No longer can the patient say, "Heal my illness, but allow me to remain the same person." From what has been said in this book, it is understandable that the new attitude originated in Palestine, during the Greek epoch. We always come upon the same turning point, "before and after Hippocrates," the transition between the Egyptian and the Greek eras, the time in which Christ asked, "Will you be healed?" and said, "Sin no more!" Humanity began to develop individuality and, at the same time, responsibility.

We have also seen, however, that the illnesses themselves have changed. Those giving us real trouble now are not the inflammations but the chronic, deformative illnesses. Here, medical treatment alone will not achieve healing in the end; the patient himself must contribute as well by changing his personality to such an extent that the illness no longer belongs to him. Many a reader may be struck by the expression that an illness "belongs" to a person. I can understand this quite well, but from the point of view from which these ideas have been conceived, it is clear that we are faced with a fundamental change in every element in the conception of humanity and nature. The word predisposition in connection with the soul life of man contained a similar thought. The expression that illness belongs to man means the same thing. How is it possible to include the patient himself in the treatment? One of the methods applied in this respect is so-called artistic therapy. Patients are advised to do artistic therapy: curative modeling, painting, music, speech, motion, etc. It is important to develop some understanding of the value of this therapy.

Let us imagine, for a moment, that someone is tuning an instrument, a piano, a violin, or a guitar. Even without having the instrument at hand, all of us will remember that two notes are struck, compared, and adjusted in the proper way to find the right pitch. The experience often begins with two notes terribly out of tune. I hope everyone remembers this horrible experience, which makes us shrink, shut our eyes, and pull a wry face. As soon as the real tone is achieved, however, we have that wonderful feeling of relaxation. Many will, just for a moment, smile unconsciously. Why? Because we experience the tuning. What does tuning mean? We are tuning the instrument in that, consciously or subconsciously, we are waiting for something to appear: a harmonious sound. We might say that tuning allows a harmony to appear.

What do we mean by harmony? Is harmony in this sense just the result of something, or is it a reality of its own? Another experience will throw some light on this little mystery. When we produce a tone on an instrument, we clearly hear it with our ears. If I produce two tones, we hear both of them. Everyone a little familiar with music knows that there is a third element that begins to be experienced: the interval. We have already mentioned this principle in the section about Paracelsus. We should not regard the interval as something that can be heard like a tone, for instance by thinking that the interval consists of the interplay of various vibrations. If this were true we could say that the third, the fourth, the fifth, and so forth, would also be audible. This is not true, however, as can clearly be demonstrated by playing two notes in sequence, taking care that the first sound has physically disappeared before producing the second one. Then everyone still has an impression of an interval. This conclusion throws a little more light on what we are trying to clarify: a piece of music does not consist of individual sounds but of intervals. Every musician will agree to this. No doubt without notes we can never experience an interval. The sounds are what we hear; yet we do not become aware of the interval through the ear; it is experienced *between* sounds.

As a melody consists of intervals, the melody opens our awareness for something that is revealed between intervals. As a symphony consists of melodies, we can go on and conclude that the reality of the symphony in its turn is experienced between the melodies. We have asked if harmony is a reality in itself. We can now ask if the interval, the melody, or the symphony, is a reality of its own?

What does a musician do when he composes music? Is he just putting different notes together, trying them out to see if they please him, or does he experience something out of other worlds that gradually begins to reveal itself, flowing easily in the case of Mozart or the result of a difficult struggle, as with Beethoven? The resulting symphony is often what people like to characterize as "divine" music. The reason for this may perhaps be found in the important realization that man, in his love for music, experiences another reality that he may deny with his thinking but may acknowledge in his heart.

I have spoken about music as the world of intervals between tones because it is the easiest example. In the same way, however, we can understand that painting reveals a "something" between colors, modeling (sculpture) a something between forms, architecture, a something between relationships of space, literature and speech, a something between words, and the art of movement, a something between movements. This summary is by no means complete and indicates merely a direction in which we must look in order to understand the "riddle" of art. Let us put these six forms of art in a diagram. Of course there are many more forms of art, but they are mainly combinations of these elementary ones.

The diagram shows surprising peculiarities. If we compare, for instance, music and architecture (architecture is often called "frozen music"), we are reminded of the relationship between the two arts shown in the word "acoustics." Furthermore, there are many similarities between the two arts. In both we have, for instance, the qualities high and low; in both we come across mathematics. This thought is not surprising when we consider the expressions we use in music for the value of a tone, that is, semitone, crotchet (1/4), quaver (1/8), semiquav-

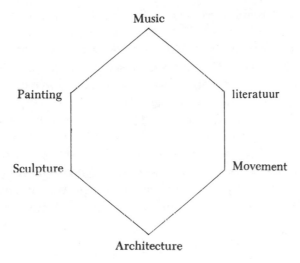

Music

Painting   literatuur

Sculpture   Movement

Architecture

er (1/16), and so forth. I know quite well that the mathematical element in music is not an exact one, but it cannot be denied. Besides, the mathematical laws in architecture are by no means really exact—except for the water level and the plumb line. The great Pythagoras was a mathematician and a musician at the same time.

We can easily find a relationship also between painting and literature. Entire languages consist of paintings or drawings only (for example, the language of North American Indian tribes or the early hieroglyphs of the Egyptians). Words and stories can picture events wonderfully, and just as music and architecture meet in acoustics, so do painting and literature meet in the illustration of books.

Sculpture and the art of movement also have a hidden, wonderful relationship. We have only to think of a statue and the living human body. The relationship is obvious. We could even call the moving human body a statue come to life.

The diagram quite unexpectedly reveals something more, however. On one side, we have sculpture and painting. Of all the arts, they most clearly have one thing in common: both show images (we need not bother about figurative or non-figurative). It is the world of the *image* in which we work. If, on the other side, we remind ourselves of the close connection between gesture and speech, if we look at the new art of movement, called eurythmy, which is called visible music but also visible speech, and we combine this with the art of literature, of speech, we have to do with two forms of art in close connection with the *word*.

At the bottom of the diagram we see the word architecture, an art that we may consider to have its origin in the *temple building* of the past. At the top is the word music, of which we have spoken already in the beginning of this chapter as a revelation of the divine element, which may remind us of an expression used earlier when speaking about Pythagoras: *the harmony of the spheres.* It was out of this realm that everything on earth came forth.

Four expressions have been used: image, word, temple, and harmony of the spheres, which may remind us of four ways in which the creation of man is expressed. Man is created out of the Word, as an image of God, as a temple of God, and out of the harmony of the spheres. We thus have discovered that the activities man displays in his different arts can be recognized in expressions used in connection with the creation of man. Man may be looked at as a work of art too, as a work of art out of the godly world, the divine, the spiritual, or the creating world, whatever we wish to call it.

If there is a grain of truth in this conclusion, a doctor who strives to heal, who strives to restore the human form, shares in a divine activity. This corresponds with what was said already in the section, "A New Impulse in Medicine." Here we should call to mind what was said in connection with the healing activity when the patient does his share in meeting the doctor by taking part in artistic therapy. A doctor must learn to understand which form of art he should apply to the particular illness. It is not possible to enter into details here.

These are, of course, quite new thoughts; people may even call it audacious to compare artistic creation with divine creation. It can be of value only if the artistic activity is done with the greatest modesty, with the greatest devotion, with the right attitude. Are not real works of art connected with sacrifice as well? Asking the patient to join the doctor in the healing process, in the restoration of the form (which is, as we have seen, a divine form), is the intention of artistic therapy, because what the patient does reacts upon his own constitution. Whether the patient, who need not be conscious of this background, can accept this sort of therapy is something else. A little example may illustrate this: a patient, a man with a managerial job, came to his doctor for treatment of a cancer. The doctor prescribed some medicine and told the patient that he should also take part in artistic therapy. The man emphatically refused. "Don't give me that nonsense," he said, "I won't do it." The doctor remained firm, however. "Sorry," he said, "The treatment involves artistic therapy, in your case painting. I cannot give you any medical treatment without your beginning the painting lessons." "Well," he said, "Then I cannot but accept." Some months later the patient visited his doctor again. After physical examination the doctor inquired, "How is the painting?" "Well," his answer was, "I told you I thought it was all nonsense, and I still think it is, but," and here he hesitated a moment, "I must agree I have discovered that I never knew what 'blue' was until now. But now I know!" It need not be much, as long as there is the beginning of a change in the human soul.

Looking at these patients, as they paint, model, and so forth, it is striking to see how they exert themselves, to see how proud they are of their results. A doctor once told me that when he saw these patients working away at something they had never done before they were so very eager that their faces glowed, and it was as if a mild fever appeared. Fever, warmth, the very element of which we are in need, just the element that modern science also has begun to discover as something of the utmost importance in cancer treatment.

The second conclusion mentioned in the beginning of this section, that the quality and choice of medicines are continually developing, concerns medicine itself. Modern medicine has the ideal of the standard remedy. As soon as we are no longer thinking of a substance with a biochemical effect, however, but of a "language" that must be understood, we can no longer stick to the ideal of uniformity. By recognizing healing qualities in certain plants, the problem is not quite solved; there still remains a distance between plant and patient. As spoken of earlier, one must be able to free the "word" (we even said, the "truth") from the plant. The plant has been called an enchantment of the word. Hahnemann introduced the use of potentized medicines. He was aware that he was not really diluting substances. The fact that he spoke of potencies implies that the more the substances were "diluted," the more they were able to display force, potency, power. Just think of the little experiment with the audience, in which I got them all to stand; this shows that weak forces can have strong results if they are understood as a "language." To free that language from the plant form is, in reality, to transfer those forces that have created that form into the diluted liquid. This is something to which we should become accustomed, the idea that we are not concerned with molecules but with freed forces in a medium, freed by diluting. It is, in fact, not easy to make these dilutions. To enter into the technique necessary to transfer *viscum album* (mistletoe), for example, into the correct medicine against cancer—its official name is Iscador*—would lead beyond the limits of this book. All I can say is that it is an incredibly complicated process. It needed many years to achieve a satisfactory result.

I would like to quote a paragraph from the work of Paracelsus. Though expressed in old-fashioned language, I believe his words can speak to our hearts.

> Nature is so careful and exact in her creation that she cannot be used without great skill, for she does not produce anything that is perfect in itself. Man must bring everything to perfection. This work of bringing things to their perfection is called "Alchemy." He is an alchemist who carries what nature grows for the use of man to its destined end. What the eye perceives in herbs or stones or trees is not yet the remedy, the eyes see only the dross.** Inside, however, beneath the dross, there the remedy lies hidden. First it must be cleansed from the dross; then it is

---

*Produced under the surveillance of the Society for Cancer Research, Arlesheim, Switzerland. There are more working societies in which scientists are striving to bring to perfection the most favorable form of preparation. The problem is a living one, by no means already solved.
**The non-essential outside.

there. This is Alchemy, and this is the office of Vulcan; he
is the apothecary and chemist of the medicine.

Is it not striking that he recognizes a divine principle to be
connected with earthly substances? Of course we are no
longer alchemists; we are doctors, but in a way doctors
must be alchemists, though no longer in hidden laboratories.

Taking all this together we can conclude that only
through preparation can a remedy really become a healing one. The main point is to feel the difference between
what has been called the modern ideal of standardized
medicines, of which the effect is known, and the medicines that are in continual development and to a high
degree adapted to the doctor's insight into the illness.
With both methods one must wait and see what the body
"is going to do with it," whether the body will accept it or
not. Both methods have their justification. A doctor must
decide freely.

Let me make a final remark. It has been stated that
medicine over the centuries gradually lost confidence in
what are now called "medical herbs." Speaking about
temple healing, we drew the conclusion, from the fact
that these treatments probably continued for thousands
of years, that they must have been effective in certain
ways. The fact that the treatment became obsolete may
well have been due to the decline in former successes.
Could it not also be that the use of herbs in early days had
results that from a certain time on caused disappointment
and therefore began to raise doubts? Having found a
means of justifying herb-application for illness as we have
described it, however, it might be that the *way* in which
the herb-substance had to be prepared needed changing.
The old-fashioned way no longer could influence the
human constitution sufficiently. The influence had to be
enhanced or strengthened.

"Strengthened," as it is meant here, however, does not mean along the path of biochemistry as it has been established in the last century. To strengthen the forces of the healing herb includes approaching the deformed body in a far more effective way, by contacting the formative forces immediately. To release the "form-speech" from its enchantment, as we have called it, is the way to strengthen the healing forces directly. This process, however, is performed in the technique of potentizing. We explained already that potentizing literally means to make stronger!

The homeopathic dilutions can indeed work more strongly than non-diluted substances because they work in another field, on another level.* In orthodox science, such thoughts are for the moment hardly acceptable; I am well aware of this. I hope, however, that out of this exploration it becomes clear that we must look for a totally new concept of illness and healing. The concept of the body of formative forces, of the life-body, must be introduced. I am convinced of this. Life should no longer be denied!

Let us turn now to our first conclusion at the beginning of this section, concerning the role of the doctor himself. The modern medical ideal is to make doctors superfluous, as we saw. I am quite sure that this must not be generalized; the trend, however, cannot be denied. That the patient is becoming more and more a number in clinics speaks for itself. This definitely should not be looked at as a criticism but as a consequence.

In our description of medicine and of the substances in the kingdoms of nature, the doctor plays an absolutely

---

*It must be emphasized that this trend of thought is not identical with the general view on the effect of high dilutions in homeopathic conceptions. We are trying to develop an entirely new approach, which is in no way based on any tradition.

essential part in the process of healing, not as someone who knows about healing but as someone who *does* the healing.* This begins to make more sense when we remind ourselves of the language that lies hidden in the plant. The doctor must apply the language of nature to the deterioration in the body. My colleague in the reported conversation (see page 93) said, "That is impossible; that is the realm of God." In a way he was right, because the doctor can heal only if he connects himself in a new way with the creating element in the world around us. It claims a very special attitude, an attitude that cannot be separated from the attitude toward the patient, from the attitude toward the process of healing, toward the applied substance. Generally, people will call this a subjective attitude, but in a way it must be subjective! This implies the opposite of the approach with standardized medicines. Two doctors may apply different herbs or metals, and both may have success.

The condition for real healing, as has been outlined in this book, is that the healing process be an extension of the doctor's activity. A doctor has the task, so to speak, of remodeling a life-body. For this he needs a mediation— the healing substance—which in a way could be described as a "lengthening" of his hands. Above all, it is essential for him to have a therapeutic conception and a therapeutic will. In taking all these facts into consideration, we must understand that they cannot be separated from the element of moral development that the person who heals has to attain, based on insight rooted in the spirit.

The three conclusions discussed in this chapter offer an answer to a critical question in modern medicine. This

---

*We should never forget that "a healing substance" is in itself an illusion. A substance cannot heal. The person, the doctor heals.

medicine triumphs in symptomatic treatments. What this
has led to can be seen in the diagram on page 88 in the
reversed arrows. The view outlined in this book sees that
total stagnation is threatening humanity's evolution. We
may call this a danger to life. A danger to life, however,
means we are threatened by death, not a physical death
but "death" in the form of materialism. The three reversed
arrows in the diagram may at the same time indicate a
turning point wherein man can find a new outlook that
leads him back to life, to light.

We can see that we are in need of a new impulse, a
need perhaps already growing stronger. An ultimate solution certainly has not yet been achieved. Perhaps the
phrase "ultimate solution" is even an illusion, because we
are not dealing with anything fixed but with insight into
therapy that must continually develop. Such an impulse
can be indicated clearly in the following. The beings in the
Egyptian era that restored the human form were called, in
the Greek era, mercurial beings, as we have mentioned
previously. We have also recognized the mercurial influence in plants and the human hand. Finally, we have
indicated that the healing activity is an activity of the
doctor that emanates from his hands.

Mercury was known as a source of healing. In the
Middle Ages, in the Rosicrucian fellowship,* Christ was
called the true Mercury. What does this mean? It means
that before and during the Greek time the initiates knew
about a spiritual being who was preparing to follow
humanity in its descent into matter. They called this being Mercury and considered Aesclepius to be directly
related to him. The early Rosicrucians recognized this being as Christ. We need not wonder, then, why Christ is

---

*Not to be confused with modern societies that may bear a similar name.

also called the Healer. In this way the unobtrusive episode of the time of Christ on earth gains new significance;
it brought an impulse which, as we have described it, had
to await its time. This time may be now and may coin-
cide with the acknowledgement that true healing can
come about only through the revelation of the being of
Christ, in and through humanity.

This healing should not be considered a miracle that
comes from without, nor as a healing by prayer but as a
daily physical deed in which this impulse can work
through the hand of the doctor. Then, to the expression
"blessed by illness" may be added *"healed by Christ"*!

Surveying the contents of this book, it becomes clear
that modern medical science as a whole has developed
parallel to man's interest in the sense world. In the beginning of this book, I indicated the great difference between consciousness as it existed before and after the time
of Hippocrates; the wisdom of the ancient times disappeared. Science began to develop toward what became
anatomy and physiology and later pathological anatomy
and the biochemistry of our times. It is interesting to see,
however, how ancient conceptions were still alive in the
nineteenth century. Rokitansky, a famous pathologist,
still developed the so-called humoral pathology, claiming
that the origin of illness consisted of a wrong composition
of blood, lymph, and the like. Does this not remind us a
little of the four liquids of Hippocrates: black gall, yellow
gall, phlegm, and blood? Rokitansky was a contemporary
of Virchov (also a famous pathologist), who rejected completely the idea of the humoral origin of illnesses. To him
the cell, the unit of living matter out of which the body in
its manifold structure was built up, was the basis of
health and illness. It was the cell in its exact appearance
that had to be studied. According to him, a thorough and

proper study of the cell, possible by microscopic investigation, would reveal all the secrets of the origin of illness.

Virchov was one of the greatest authorities of his time. His conviction worked so powerfully that Rokitansky, who was highly impressed by him, hardly dared read his own writings any longer. We should not think, however, that Virchov was just a dry scholar. Virchov's opinion was that if something is not clear one should look at it, study it in every detail, and eventually one will be able to discover its secret.* This idea could just as well have been expressed by Goethe. We can hardly find greater scientific differences than between Virchov and Goethe, yet they have two things in common: conviction and enthusiasm.

Science on the whole had to develop in the way it has developed. Whether the consequence of Virchov's thinking in the field of *medical* science has been favorable to medicine is another story. The consequences that began to appear after the beginning of this century were based on Virchov's discoveries and have since developed further into what has become our modern medicine. The world into which the development of man's consciousness has led is the world of physical evidence. Both Virchov and Goethe lived in this world.

In the introductory section we considered the transition from the old consciousness into that of our own time, taking Hippocrates' time as the turning point. What has been said about Aristotle, the first scientist in the modern sense of the word, about the old lady to whom I said that the world we perceive is "the outside of God," about Pico della Mirandola, who said that God had created man to see Him and to love Him—all these images merge to illustrate the transition.

---

*Verbrugh, *Medicine on the Wrong Track.*

But what *are* our senses in reality? Goethe said, "The eye has been created by and for the light." This has no meaning for the exact sciences. To Virchov, such information had no scientific value at all. Is it wise, however, to reject a statement like Goethe's completely? What does this statement include? A common phenomenon can put us on the track to find the answer to this question: the similarity between the human eye and the camera. Let us look at the camera and ask a few questions.

Why is there a lens in front of the camera? Because otherwise the light would not project pictures. Why is the inside of the camera black? Because otherwise the light would produce false reflections. Why is there a diaphragm? Because otherwise the light would not be able to produce sharp outlines in the picture. Why is there a shutter? Because otherwise the light would affect the sensitive sheet too intensely. Four times we come across the word "light" as the subject of the sentence.

In making the camera, man had to follow the laws of the light! It is eventually the light that dictated the construction. We can draw the conclusion that the camera is made by man but constructed by the light. Hence the similarity with the eye. The body has built an organ, the construction of which is dictated by the laws of the light! If the light has created the eye, we should not forget that light itself is invisible, even from a scientific point of view. What we see are colors only, but the colors too have been described by Goethe in a very special way. His description was that colors are the deeds and sufferings of the light. We could put these two statements of Goethe's into one sentence: an invisible light has created the eye in order to make its deeds and sufferings visible. We could also use a similar formula for the other organs of sense. For instance, for the ear: an inaudible sound has created the ear to make its deeds and sufferings heard. This parallels the relationship between light and color. Are we not, in speaking of inaudible sounds, reminded of the expression, "the harmony of the spheres," used by every major figure from Plato to Kepler to indicate a special aspect of the creative, divine world? We should never forget that a certain intuitive knowledge of ancient wisdom has always remained with humanity, has perhaps never totally disappeared.

Let us, finally, without hesitation, apply our formula to the whole world of the senses and say: an imperceptible world has created our senses to perceive its deeds and sufferings. Again we can picture man facing the outside of the spiritual world in his environment, able to see it and to love it. Here we have made a transition from the world of exactness into that of "inactness" (see page   ). The world of exactness is the same as the created world; the world of "inactness" is the creating one, the world of the spiritual beings.

The next problem is to determine what a consideration like the previous one means to us. Are we touched by it, and if so, to which element in us does it appeal? In my estimation, there lives in everyone a something, a principle, which is in danger of being forgotten, which has been lost from sight, which maybe *had* to be forgotten in order to become fully immersed in the world of differentiation. In reality we are distinguishing the divine world in its perceptibility, in its deeds and sufferings, by the fact that we have learned to differentiate.

The principle of which I spoke just now, which, though hidden and small, still lives in everyone and shows itself in the longing for a return to an awareness of the spiritual world, of the divine element, is at the same time the principle I meant when I asked, what touches our heart, what enables us to be enthusiastic about a new conception of the world around us? Do we not see tendencies and inclinations everywhere for people to turn away from the world of exactness, in which the human soul often does not find sufficient nourishment? Is it not time that the mentioned "little principle," the Little Prince in us, come again to claim its rights? Why has the remark of the creator of *The Little Prince*, Antoine de Saint-Exupéry, "The essential is invisible to the eye," given satisfaction to so many souls?

I hope it is clear that I attribute an equal value to the enthusiasm of a scientist like Virchov. The question is, however, in which direction are his statements leading us? We should not forget that there is a straight line from Virchov's conception of the human body to the computer medicine of our time. If a doctor knows all the symptoms of an illness and all the other facts and conditions, the computer will indicate the proper medicine in each particular case. We would thus have achieved the utmost ideal of exactness.

In calling this section of the book "Conditions for Healing in the Future," we have expressed the polar opposite. Medicine, patient, and doctor must be seen as being in continual evolution. I do not mean to say that the ideal of computer medicine is already general opinion; I am convinced that many modern doctors would most definitely reject such an idea as an ideal. Have we not experienced, however, that so many things we would not have thought possible some thirty years ago, for instance, legal abortion, are discussed openly now and desired by thousands of people? Do we not feel that we must continually accept matters that we would have thought unacceptable not so long ago? Are we not on a certain path, and do we not have to discover the direction in which we are going?

This leads us back to the outset of this book. To shift away from the world of exactness should not mean to lose exactness entirely. On the contrary, only by the fact that we have learned to differentiate in the sense world are we able to recognize the related reality in the spiritual world.

Many years ago I entered upon a discussion about a similar problem with a friend of mine who was a surgeon. He kindly but emphatically rejected every suggestion about a world beyond that of the senses, saying, "I wish to remain with both feet on the ground." My answer was, "That is exactly my wish too, but I have the impression that you, and many modern scientists, are standing not only with your feet but also with your heads on the ground! I favor another ideal: feet on the ground, head in heaven!"* It is clear that such an expression can be understood in the proper way only when we have gone along the path of thought. If such an expression like "feet on the ground, head in heaven" is taken in the right sense, however, we can feel as though freed from fetters.

One can, of course, assume that man's existence is limited by birth and death. One can take it for granted that illness is a combination of symptoms caused by influences from without. One can then easily appreciate the thought that the symptoms of illnesses should be fought until they are overcome. I consider it important for everyone to try to think this over seriously. Can we in such a way, however, feel that life has sense, has a meaning? One should then try to think the other way round, considering man's life between birth and death as a temporary but necessary link in the stream of evolution. One should try to consider illness as a possibility to eliminate

---

*Previously we used the expression, reaching for the height, remaining firmly on the ground.

the blocking predisposition, which one has created through life on earth. One should try to see healing as an activity that does not fight the illness but that takes over its task in the appropriate way.

Both visions strive to save life, no doubt; the second vision, however, is not without a condition. That condition is that the body, the instrument in which man must pursue his evolution, be kept as transparent as possible.

A Recapitulation

Looking back at the history of medicine, aware of the crucial time in which we live despite great materialistic successes, we can make the following summary. Medicine fights symptoms of illnesses. The illness, which shows itself in the symptoms, originates in the formative principle, whose activity results in the totality of the human shape, the human form. The origin of the visible symptoms lies in a deformation of that formative principle that we have called the life-body. The idea of "life" as a reality was thereby introduced anew. The deformation in its turn has its origin in the life of the soul of man.

The change in the "mystery of illness" in the course of time lies in the change and in the increase of the symptoms. Humanity's constitution, physical and psychical, underwent a strong influence as a result of the change of consciousness. This change is part of humanity's evolution. The symptoms caused by our environment, which became more and more materialistically inclined, continually claimed a new approach. Modern methods have been called "violent" in this book. I think nobody can deny the correctness of that expression, especially when we think of the increase of side effects or aftereffects. On the other hand, no one should shut his eyes to the fact that the modern treatments are a logical consequence of the increase in the seriousness of the symptoms. Tumors, heart attacks, deterioration of the central nervous system, rheumatic deformations: in all areas, humanity suffers more than ever before. Medicine's answer, to "fight" symptoms as we have called it, is a natural consequence.

In doing this, however, the doctors have become fascinated, so to speak, by these facts; they have been drawn or tempted to search for the true nature of illness in the world of perception only. Biochemistry, following the symptomatical deterioration into the depths of the tissues, the histological structure, has lost sight of the beginning point. It has tried to solve the problem of the origin of illness from the wrong end.

Hence our question: "Are we on the right path?" The answer clearly is: *no*. We need not deny the treatment of symptoms, as has been said so often in this book, but the moment doctors expect by this treatment to overcome illness itself, medicine goes astray. Humanity has forgotten the essential, being so taken in by the strong impressions of the non-essential. This is the reason I have introduced the thought that after Hippocrates medicine gradually began to forget about healing.

Healing is a restoration of the form. In ancient Egypt, this restoration took place through the direct influence of the creative world itself. In that world, however, the source of healing must be found. As far as inflammations are concerned, we still must recognize the miracle of cosmic healing. Medicine is blind to this fact, mesmerized, as it were, by the fact that it could prevent inflammations, unaware that it often attacked the healing process at the same time! In the case of noninflammatory illnesses, illnesses without warmth, where there is no heightened activity of the formative forces, of the life-body, medicine must take over the task of healing. The doctor, as the healer, must find the way toward restoration of the deformation, meeting the ailment from without, with the help of what the earth offers. This makes it necessary to develop a totally new vision regarding the kingdoms of nature. We may say, "From healing heaven to helping earth."

A change of attitude toward the phenomenon of illness itself is necessary. Symptoms must be understood, not merely combated. As soon as we recognize the value of the symptoms (generally called "the illness"), by taking away the predisposition, the slogan, "Illness should not be," ceases to make sense. Illness, in spite of the paradox, blesses humanity by making possible his evolution. He who denies evolution denies the true element in humanity. Even by doing away with the symptoms, we should develop the "attitude" not of fighting but of taking over the task of the illness. This attitude will prevent us from having the illusion that violence has any claim to being the right method.

We can come to a deep understanding through the following suggestion. In summing up the moments in which we came upon examples of real healing, we must think of:

— the temple sleep in Egypt and Greece
— fever
— the application of plants
— laying on of hands, anticipating so to speak, the healings of Christ.

We have introduced the name Mercury as an expression given to healing divine forces. This enables us to combine these four examples. The question has been asked, has the fact that the god Mercury was considered a healer anything to do with the qualities of the metal mercury? We have already touched on this question regarding the healing qualities of mistletoe.

In the metal *mercury* we discovered:

Mercury

Warmth	Image of Respiration	Cosmic Aspect
(liquid metal)	(dispersion and concentration)	(dissolving metals)
(hidden)	(hidden)	(hidden)

The description gave us a notion of the qualities for which we had to look in the case of healing.

Fever gives us clearest evidence of helping mercurial activity:

Fever

Warmth	Image of Respiration	Cosmic Aspect
(revealed)	(revealed)	(revealed)

The *plant* or the herb approaches the illness in a different way:

Plant

Warmth	Image of Respiration	Cosmic Aspect
(revealed in coal, oil, and gas, originally stemming from the sun)	(revealed in the threefold rhythm of expansion and contraction in the qualities of the leaves from the roots to the top)	(revealed in the form of the plant stretching from earth to heaven)

The herb as a medicine, however, does not come "from heaven" as fever does; it must be prescribed, must be applied manually by a human being.

In early times the laying on of hands was practiced as a direct influence on the life-body of the patient. We have shown that this was possible only long ago when conditions were different, when the patients, as well as he who healed, were themselves much different from the way they are now. We said that they were far more open. The real example of this healing was given in the healings of Christ. The moment Christ laid His hands on someone (we need not ponder over the fact that Christ's influence and activity were not always the same), we meet a union of "heaven and hand."

Should modern medicine not strive in the same direction? In our hands also we find a "cosmic tendency." With our hands we are active not only in the realm of the earth but also in the realm of the spirit. In lifting things, we free them from the force of gravity. In our movements, in the art of gesture, we bring together the life of our hands with the spiritual activities of thinking and speaking. The fingers of our hands can be spread out or clenched into a fist; we have seen that we are able to contract and to expand with our hands, a remarkable example of rhythmic alternation. Our hands reveal wonderful mercurial qualities. Regarding the third element, the warmth element, it is not difficult to find the answer. Warmth, in using our hands, should be understood as love. Love is not a feeling in the first place; love is a force, a force of goodness and compassion, which can flow into our deeds and actions:

Hands

Warmth (Love)	Image of Respiration (Opening and Closing)	Cosmic Aspect (In the service of spiritual life)

The entire industry of medicinal preparations, the hundreds of activities necessary in laboratories, factories, apothecaries, and so forth, should work with an awareness of the only aim: healing. This is not an illusion; the improvement of a medicine that has been described previously must go hand in hand with a development in the field of the production of medicines, by looking at healing as an ideal closely connected with feelings of respect for our fellow men. And the doctor, who is the mediator between medicine and patient, can fulfill his task in the proper way only if he is conscious, continually conscious, of the greatness of his profession: to represent healing on earth.

The medicine that can heal the deformation in the life-body is an extension of the healing activity of the doctor. His therapeutic conception, his will for healing, his love for the human being, issue, radiate from that element in him of which we are reminded by the words of St. Paul, "Not I, but Christ in me." I previously offered a special sentence, and I may now add a last phrase to it, thinking of humanity with its ailments and sorrows:

Blessed by illness, healed by Christ in us!

VI

Epilogue

In looking back over the book I would like, for a moment, to share a personal experience. Years ago, I treated an elderly lady who suffered from cancer. The tumor had grown extensively throughout her body. She was in the final phase. Before dying, she had lain silent and immobile for a period of three weeks, without taking any food. Her son, an old friend of mine, and I visited her several times a day. By good fortune she did not suffer greatly but quietly passed away. The remarkable impression I had throughout these three weeks was of a great change coming over her. She became more interested in her environment than before; she became amiable and tolerant; in greeting us, she smiled in a touching way, which gave me the strong impression that the little part of her body in which she could still live became more and more "transparent." I said to her son, "In spite of the fact that she will soon die, I have the feeling that she is undergoing a healing process at the same time; that little part of her body in which she still 'resides' seems to be growing continually more healthy, as if losing its deformation!"

After I had seen her the last time, while driving home, the picture of the mystery of humanity and illness stood before me. I kept in mind that impression of transparency, which had taught me to consider the human being as a spiritual being, living in the dwelling that enables it to evolve. I imagined all of us continually causing divinely created deformations, which are taken from us by the "blessing" of illness. I pondered further that there is a mystery in healing as well, which in reality signifies joining in the godly activity of restoring our human form. I also had to think about the seriousness of striving to be worthy to perform such a healing activity. For it means that we ourselves in so doing carry the source of healing in ourselves, a source of maintenance and restoration, a source of the divine creative activity on earth.

"God is dead," people say. If so, does that mean that we must look for the divine on earth? I think that is the point, to recognize the divine in its very real presence "here," in humanity itself. In every human being lives something, often very hidden, often denied, often nearly suffocated, but never really absent. If it shows itself, it may be recognized by its smallness, which means its modesty, by its openness to the needs of others. It is this little principle that must be born in us in order to be able to heal.

For me that special book I mentioned earlier, one that has brought warmth and light to so many hearts, St.-Exupéry's *The Little Prince*, contains the key to the human riddle. What Antoine de St.-Exupéry was trying to tell humanity, using the image of the sheep (the lamb), the snake, the thorns, the desert, and the well, etc., ending with ascension, may signify the recognition of a new light in the human being. May this light begin to radiate more and more. Though we are only at the beginning, the prospects for the future, it seems, are open.

Bibliography

J.H. van den Berg, *Medische macht en medische etiek.* Nijkerk, The Netherlands: Callenbach, 1969.

Joh. van Beverwijck, *Van de genees-konste en de heel-konste.* Amsterdam: 1651.

F.A. Bol, "Alternatieve geneeswijzen," *Medisch Contact.* 1978.

Louis Bolk, *Hersenen en cultur.* Amsterdam: Scheltema en Holkema, 1918.

"Carcinoombehandeling," articles in *Nederlands Tijdschrift voor Geneeskunde.* 1980.

Rudolf Herzog, *Die Wunderheilungen von Epidauros.* N.p.: Beitrag zur Geschichte der Medizin und Religion, n.d.

Malcolm Julke, *Encyclopedie van alternatieve geneeskunde.* 1978.

Paul Hühnerfeld, *Kleine Geschichte der Medizin.* Gütersloh: Signum, n.d.

L.B.W. Jongkees, "Zijn wij op de goede weg?" *Nederlands Tijdschrift voor Geneeskunde.* 1977.

Tine Kaayk, "Een Bijzondere Praktijkervaring," *Arts en Wereld.* 1978.

L.F.C. Mees, *The Dressed Angel.* London and New York: Regency Press, 1975.

_____, *Living Metals: Relationship between Man and Metals.* London and New York: Regency Press, 1974.

Giovanni Pico della Mirandola, *On the Dignity of Man.* Indianapolis: Bobbs-Merrill, 1965.

Desmond Morris, *The Naked Ape.* New York: McGraw-Hill, 1967.

Wilhelm Pelikan, *The Secrets of Metals.* Trans., Charlotte Lebensart. Spring Valley, N.Y.: Anthroposophic Press, 1973.

F. van Soeren, "De tragedie van de zeventiger jaren," *Medisch Contact.* 1978.

Rudolf Steiner, *Von Seelenrätseln.* Dornach, Switzerland: Philosophisch-Anthroposophischer Verlag, 1917. (Partially translated by Owen Barfield as *The Case for Anthroposophy.* London: Rudolf Steiner Press, 1970.)

_____, *De wetenschap van de geheimen der ziel.* Zeist, The Netherlands: Vrij Geestesleven, 1980.

Mellie Uyldert, *De Taal der Kruiden.* Naarden, The Netherlands: Strengholt, 1972.

H.S. Verbrugh, *Geneeskunde op dood spoor.* Rotterdam: Lemniscaat, 1974.

FOR FURTHER READING
Five Basic Books

Rudolf Steiner intended these carefully written volumes to serve as a foundation to all of the later, more advanced anthroposophical writings and lecture courses.

THE PHILOSOPHY OF FREEDOM by Rudolf Steiner. "Is human action free?" asks Steiner in his most important philosophical work. By first addressing the nature of knowledge, Steiner cuts across the ancient debate of real or illusory human freedom. A painstaking examination of human experience as a polarity of percepts and concepts shows that only in thinking does one escape the compulsion of natural law. Steiner's argument arrives at the recognition of the self-sustaining, universal reality of thinking that embraces both subjective and objective validity. Free acts can be performed out of love for a "moral intuition" grasped ever anew by a living thinking activity. Steiner scrutinizes numerous world-views and philosophical positions and finally indicates the relevance of his conclusions to human relations and life's ultimate questions. As he later pointed out, the sequence of thoughts in this book can also become a path toward spiritual knowledge.

(226 pp) Paper, $5.50 #116

KNOWLEDGE OF THE HIGHER WORLDS AND ITS ATTAINMENT by Rudolf Steiner. Rudolf Steiner's fundamental work on the path to higher knowledge explains in detail the exercises and disciplines a student must pursue in order to attain a wakeful experience of super-sensible realities. The stages of Preparation, Enlightenment, and Initiation are described, as is the transformation of dream life and the meeting with the Guardian of the Threshold. Moral exercises for developing each of the spiritual lotus petal organs ("chakras") are given in accordance with the rule of taking three steps in moral development for each step into spiritual knowledge. The path described here is a safe one which will not interfere with the student's ability to lead a normal outer life.

(237 pp) Paper, $6.95 #80; Cloth, $14.00 #363

*THEOSOPHY, AN INTRODUCTION TO THE SUPER-SENSIBLE KNOWLEDGE OF THE WORLD AND THE DESTINATION OF MAN by Rudolf Steiner. In this work Steiner carefully explains many of the basic concepts and terminologies of anthroposophy. The book begins with a sensitive description of the primordial trichotomy: body, soul, and spirit, elaborating the various higher members of the human constitution. A discussion of reincarnation and karma follows. The next and longest chapter (75 pages) presents, in a vast panorama, the seven regions of the soul world, the seven regions of the land of spirits, and the soul's journey after death through these worlds. A brief discussion of the path to higher knowledge follows. "Read... Rudolf Steiner's little book on theosophy—your hair will stand on end!" (Saul Bellow in *Newsweek*)

(395 pp) Paper, $6.95 #155; Cloth, $9.95 #154

*CHRISTIANITY AND OCCULT MYSTERIES OF ANTIQUITY by Rudolf Steiner. An introduction to esoteric Christianity which explores the ancient mythological wisdom of Egypt and Greece. The work shows how this wisdom underwent a tremendous transformation into a historical event in the mystery of Golgotha. Formerly published as *Christianity as Mystical Fact.*

(241 pp)   Cloth, $14.00 #662; Paper, $7.95 #33

*OCCULT SCIENCE, AN OUTLINE by Rudolf Steiner. This work of nearly 400 pages begins with a thorough discussion and definition of the term "occult" science. A description of the supersensible nature of the human being follows, along with a discussion of dreams, sleep, death, life between death and rebirth, and reincarnation. In the fourth chapter evolution is described from the perspective of initiation science. The fifth chapter characterizes the training a student must undertake as a preparation for initiation. The sixth and seventh chapters consider the future evolution of the world and more detailed observations regarding supersensible realities.

(388 pp)   Paper, $6.95 #113; Cloth, $10.95 #112

On Rudolf Steiner and Anthroposophy

RUDOLF STEINER: HERALD OF A NEW EPOCH by Stewart C. Easton. Dr. Easton's interest in Rudolf Steiner dates from 1934, and he has been involved in anthroposophical activities in one way or another ever since. A historian by profession, Dr. Easton brings together in this book innumerable facts and details of Steiner's life that have been previously unavailable to English readers. The result is an outstanding portrait of a unique personality that will satisfy a long-felt need.

(376 pp)   Paper, $10.95 #427

MAN AND WORLD IN THE LIGHT OF ANTHROPOSOPHY by Stewart C. Easton. A new and revised edition of Dr. Easton's survey of Rudolf Steiner's anthroposophy. This comprehensive "textbook" complete with index includes chapters on the historical evolution of human consciousness, individual spiritual development, karma, the arts, the Waldorf school movement, Biodynamic agriculture, medicine and nutrition, the sciences, and more. Provides "the reader with an appreciation of the enormous wealth and richness of what Steiner gave to mankind. It serves admirably as an introduction to Steiner's work as a whole." *(The Book Exchange)*

(536 pp)   Cloth, $21.00 #353

On Health and Illness

HEALTH AND ILLNESS VOL. 1 by Rudolf Steiner. The nine lectures in this volume are part of the lectures given to the workmen at the first Goetheanum. Steiner discusses such topics as the illnesses specific to life phases, the formation of the human ear, the thyroid and hormones, treatments for mental and physical rejuvenation, the eye and hair color, the nose, smell and taste, the soul life and the breathing process, and why we become sick. The pictures of the human organism are so clear, vivid and full of insight that they should be of interest both to the layman and the medical professional.

(155 pp)   Paper, $7.95 #68; Cloth, $12.95 #174

THE ANTHROPOSOPHICAL APPROACH TO MEDICINE, VOL. 1 established by Friedrich Husemann, newly edited and revised by Otto Wolff, with contributions from eight others. This first volume of a projected four-volume medical text translated from the German and written out of the approach of Rudolf Steiner's anthroposophy will prove invaluable to medical practitioners seeking a concrete understanding of the body's relationship to soul and spirit. The readable text is also comprehensible to the interested layman. This volume includes an extensive section on developmental disorders and diseases of childhood and adolescence, followed by treatments of hysteria and neurasthenia, the polarities of inflammation and sclerosis, the biochemistry and pathology of nutrition and human metabolism, the pharmaceutical science of healing plants, and the "capillary-dynamic" and "sensitive crystallization" blood tests as diagnostic tools.

(414 pp, illus.)   Cloth, $30.00 #636

OVERCOMING NERVOUSNESS by Rudolf Steiner (Munich, 1912). Practical advice for strengthening the memory and will, and directions for overcoming nervous tension. From these exercises a new inner strength is developed making it possible for the individual to better face present social conditions.

(19 pp)   Paper, $1.50 #114

PROBLEMS OF NUTRITION by Rudolf Steiner. Steiner treats from a spiritual outlook the digestive process, vegetable and animal protein, and the effects of alcohol, coffee, tea, and milk. (Munich, Jan. 8, 1909)

(22 pp)   Paper, $2.00 #124

SENSITIVE CRYSTALLIZATION PROCESSES—A DEMONSTRATION OF FORMATIVE FORCES IN THE BLOOD by Ehrenfried Pfeiffer. This important work contains 4 drawings and 26 photographic plates. It covers the technique of producing the crystallizations, used in medical blood tests and food quality testing, and discusses different experiments performed by Pfeiffer and his co-workers.

(59 pp)   Paper, $12.95 #434